Catherine Mabe

ROLLER DERBY

THE HISTORY AND ALL-GIRL REVIVAL OF THE GREATEST SPORT ON WHEELS

speck press
denver

Published by: speck press, speckpress.com

ISBN 13: 978-1-933108-11-7
ISBN 10: 1-933108-11-8

Book layout and design by: **CORVUS**, corvusdesignstudio.com

Printed and bound in Mexico

Library of Congress Cataloging-in-Publication Data
Mabe, Catherine.
  Roller derby : the greatest sport on wheels from the Great Depression to the all-female revival / by Catherine Mabe.
     p. cm.
   ISBN-13: 978-1-933108-11-7 (pbk. : alk. paper)
   ISBN-10: 1-933108-11-8 (pbk. : alk. paper)
  1. Roller derbies--United States. 2. Roller skating--United States. 3. Roller skaters--United States. I. Title.
GV859.6.M33 2006
796.21--dc22
                              2006029512

10 9 8 7 6 5 4 3 2 1

To my ma, for never saying, "You're going to do what?"

ACKNOWLEDGMENTS

Thanks first and foremost to Denver's finest, the Rocky Mountain Rollergirls. I am proud to know you.

My gratitude and heart to Paul Perez, Amanda Gagliardi, Jen Frale, Heather Dalton, Misti Dawn Patterson, Autumn Hebener, Darlene Coffin, Amy Larson, April O'Hare, Shannon Boyles, Shelley Koehn, Jen Wilson, Denise Grimes, Janet Clarke, Michelle Baldwin, Jon Mullett, Jim Denes, Chris Jankosky, and Lupe Cantu.

I am most grateful to the legends who brought this sport to life. We remember.

And thanks to all of the photographers, skaters, and support staff who so willingly contributed a piece of themselves to this book, all for the love of derby. And to the fans across the world who are part of the derby experience.

Thanks to everyone at Speck Press for understanding the derby way.

Appreciation also to my employers past and present for helping me afford the bearings, wheels, skates, and pink terry cloth tracksuit required to live my double life.

CONTENTS

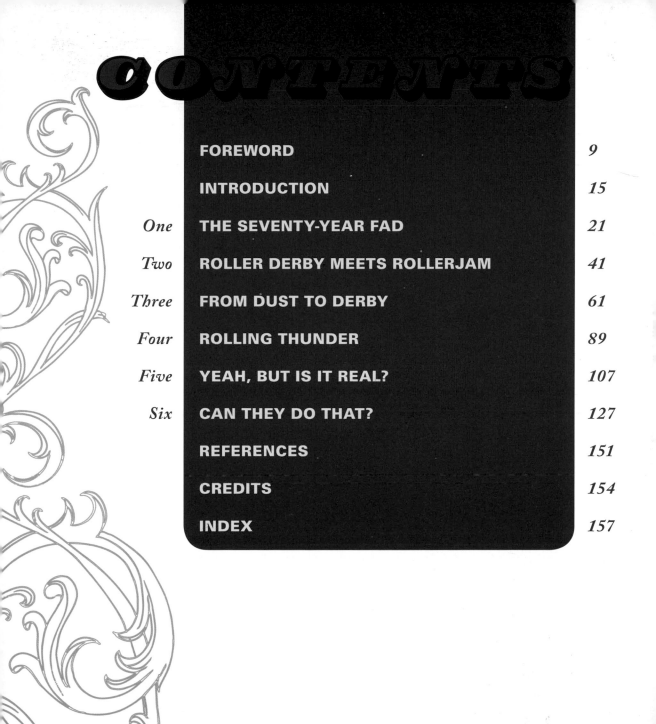

FOREWORD

"Where do I start?" I ask.

"*Your* story," Jayne—Catherine—explains.

I realize it's my story she's asking for, but not because I'm special; it's because, in a sense, derby stories are universal. Mine might differ in the details and timeline, but it has some pretty common factors with every derby girl out there.

My first memory of roller derby formed the summer before I started high school. I was up late, flipping through channels, and stumbled on *RollerGames*, the eighties comeback of roller derby. I stopped to watch the show because I was a big Blondie fan, and she was the musical guest that night. I was a faithful viewer the rest of that summer. But when school started I couldn't stay up that late anymore, and shortly after that it went off the air.

I never forgot about roller derby, though, and years later for my birthday a very dear friend gave me a movie poster from *Unholy Rollers*, a seminal B-movie from the seventies. I hung it at the end of my couch and found myself daydreaming daily about derby. The illustration of the beautiful, angry girl bulldozing through the pack, with women flying in every direction in the wake of her pass…it was me. Or at least I wanted it to be me. I had never played sports—hated them, in fact. But I couldn't stop picturing myself in that scene.

I was already thirty then. I'd played in a few bands, written a few fanzines, and raised myself in the punk-rock scene, where it's a short jump from wishing you can do something to deciding you're going to just do it. So it wasn't long before I found myself on a local music message board posting, *Who Wants to Join My Roller Derby Team?* I didn't know much about derby and I couldn't even find a copy of the rules, but I knew I could figure it out. So just like starting a band, I recruited girls and we met over pitchers of beer to strategize our derby venture. Three months later we played our first bout.

I have a video of that bout, but I can't watch it. I cringe just thinking of it now. We must have been so bad. But we were lucky: it was 2003 and no one in Arizona had seen derby in so long that our enthusiasm carried us a really long way. We had no idea what we were doing, but we knew the principles: the jammer scores by passing opponents and everyone but the jammer is there to stop the opposing jammer or help their own jammer get by, that and it's all done on roller skates. Armed with that knowledge and rink rental skates, we sold out our first bout and managed to have a total blast without breaking our legs or anyone else's.

Since then the thrill of that first night has developed into a lasting love of game details and strategy we couldn't have ever imagined. Our ranks are mixed with girls who've never played sports and girls who've played every sport under the sun. While it may be the short skirts and furious contact that brings in the fans (and new players), I think it's the strategy and pure love of the game that's obvious in every skater that keeps them coming back.

But back to my story…that first bout in November 2003 brought like-minded women out of the woodwork. Phoenix became the second city to host a derby league (it only took a

week to figure out if we wanted to play we'd have to have more than one team!), and with help from our sisters in Austin, who'd been playing more than a year, we quickly scheduled a bout every month. Girls from Los Angeles came to see us play and went back to tell their newly formed league what they saw. The founder of the LA Derby Dolls told her best friend in New York about what they were doing, and the Gotham Girls were born. Word spread like wildfire.

Now, less than three short years later, what was a handful of teams now numbers well over a hundred leagues and growing worldwide, most with four teams or more.

I'm in my second league now, founded in Las Vegas with a skater from Arizona—my archenemy, in fact, the captain of my former team's biggest rival in Arizona Roller Derby (AZRD). After our championship game in 2005, we joined forces in Las Vegas to start a new team with one goal: let's skate all the time and play every team we possibly can. Since then, our quad skates have been rolling over state lines across the nation, with crowd-packed venues welcoming us at every turn.

Sometimes I ask myself if the derby honeymoon will last forever. For me, I think so. Even after I retire from actively playing (which can't happen until my team beats a Texas Rollergirls' team), I will still coach, still talk about all-things derby, and still be involved long after my hips seize up, my knees give out, and my wheels stop rolling. And that's what this book is about: that true love that doesn't fade and the enduring, inspiring legacy of a sport started more than seventy years ago.

My day job: derby; my love life: a derby leaguemate. Even my vacations, as rare as they are, are spent traveling to other cities to

skate or coach derby. A week doesn't go by that I don't learn and love something new about derby. I eat, sleep, and dream it, and I couldn't be happier.

—From Fabulous Las Vegas,
proud home of the Neander Dolls and Sin City Rollergirls,
Ivanna S. Pankin, #22

INTRODUCTION

"Derby changed my life."

It's the most common quote, bar none, you'll hear from derby folks old and new, male and female, banked and flat. This sport irreversibly alters a person, and, in many cases, saves them. That's certainly been the case for me.

I've been hired and fired because I'm a derby girl. I've lost love and found it, courtesy of derby. I've been invited in and kicked out, and I've gone from anti-jock to full-fledged paint-my-face-pink-and-scream-until-it-hurts sports fan. All because of derby.

It all started innocently enough. I attended the first practice of Denver's Rocky Mountain Rollergirls sporting those brown suede numbers with orange wheels—the same rental skates in heavy rotation in rinks around the country. I put them on, laced them up, and immediately worried about how I'd navigate the restroom let alone the rink. It had been a long time since I was on wheels—since my fifth-grade birthday, as a matter of fact. Fortunately, most of the other women were in the same boat. So I threw caution to the wind and hobbled embarrassingly around the rink.

After skating, we all sat down to discuss derby names, team themes, and how to grow our ranks. We did all this with little acknowledgment that we, in that moment, were part of history. We simply wanted to bring derby fever to Colorado.

The rink quickly became the nucleus surrounding a passion unparalleled. It was the site of so many practices and strategy sessions and the laughs, arguments, and meetings that go along with it all. It was our practice space and our office. It was home.

I soon realized I was happiest on the rink. Life on the outside began to dim a little as those who weren't roller girls found it harder and harder to participate in conversations with me. I could turn any discussion into one about derby. I wanted opinions on bearings, wheels, and which skates to buy—not exactly typical watercooler chit chat. My wardrobe changed, as well. Several pairs of fishnet stockings and a pink terry cloth tracksuit (the official uniform of the Rocky Mountain Rollergirls' Sugar Kill Gang) filled out my closet. Suddenly, all of my friends were on eight wheels. And I couldn't have been happier about it.

I went to practice, slowly got my skate legs, and worked through the intricacies of actually playing the game with the other girls who showed up each week. We trained hard and progressed. I started getting knocked around, getting scared, becoming brave, taking hits, dealing blows…the whole time thinking, *Me, an athlete? Me, playing a team sport?*

Yup, this was me doing all of this, and I wasn't alone. I was surrounded by more opinionated, vocal, strong, wise, competitive, and genuine women than I ever knew existed. They were willing to put in the time to learn the sport, find coaches and sponsors, track down a venue to bout, catch the eye of the press, recruit skaters, and complete the other multitude of tasks that keep all-women, DIY derby leagues afloat. And they did it while running households, working bread-and-butter jobs, taking care of loved ones, and doing everything else that goes along with life.

Although logging too many hours to count, we retained our sense of humor and love of the sport. It says a lot about folks when they can ride out the bumps in the road inherent in being part of a group and still maintain their commitment level and sanity. And I love what it says about *Rocky Mountain Rollergirls*: we are as dedicated as ever to roller derby and have overcome some hurdles we never could have imagined being placed in front of us.

Looking beyond Denver's city limits, we eventually hit the road. Arriving in Las Vegas, we played our inaugural interleague bout against the Sin City Rollergirls. I had never experienced such a swell of pride; we'd made so much happen, and we'd done it on our own terms.

From the women in Austin who started this brand of the revolution to the newly forming teams in Germany and London, derby lives on. And it gets better with each evolution, or, rather, revolution. Rules continue to be debated and tightened, the play is getting faster and harder, interleague play is becoming more fierce, and derby skaters and fans everywhere are having more and more fun as a result.

I only hope that those just embarking on this long road have as much fun as I had and continue to have. I've been hip checked by the legendary Lorretta "Little Iodine" Behrens, one of derby's greatest historical names. I've roller skated in my old-school quads down Denver's longest and wickedest street, Colfax Avenue. Hades Lady of TXRD Lonestar Rollergirls, the best of the best, taught me how to enter the banked track and how to safely flip over the railing head first. I've played a sport wearing head-to-toe pink terry cloth regalia in front of thousands

Denver's Rocky Mountain Rollergirls was established in 2004. (above and left)

of people! And I've sat with a legend of times past, Gloria "Gorgeous Gloria" Bent, who assured me there is life after derby. (Yet, I'm still not convinced.)

I've also made friends who understand me in ways no one else ever will. These dear soulmates' couches are strewn across the nation and available to me whenever my wheels and I need a travel destination. What derby lacks in glamour it makes up for in spades by the benefits of being part of the sisterhood of those doing it. The guarantee of a place to lay my head and the promise of always having someone to skate with me may not seem like much to some, but to me it's solid gold.

I wrote this book to share a little piece of that gold, to pull back the curtain and reveal that with derby, as is true with many great things, there is so much more than meets the eye. There's no other sport in the world like it, and that fact shouldn't be relegated purely to the knowledge of roller girls. Derby takes hold of you and never lets go, whether you're a roller girl, a fan, or support staff.

In short, I want to unlock the mystery that is roller derby, to show the world who the skaters of the past and present are, how strong our ties bind, how literally crazed we can all be, and how gripped we are by this sport. And I want people to know how plain fun, exhilerating, and addictive bouts are.

—Catherine "Jayne Manslaughter" Mabe,
Sugar Kill Gang team member for life,
Denver, Colorado

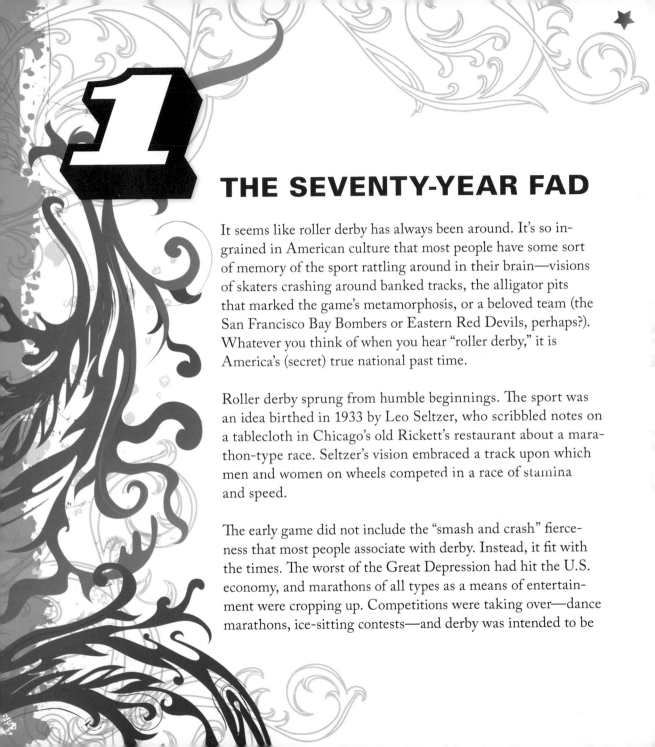

1

THE SEVENTY-YEAR FAD

It seems like roller derby has always been around. It's so ingrained in American culture that most people have some sort of memory of the sport rattling around in their brain—visions of skaters crashing around banked tracks, the alligator pits that marked the game's metamorphosis, or a beloved team (the San Francisco Bay Bombers or Eastern Red Devils, perhaps?). Whatever you think of when you hear "roller derby," it is America's (secret) true national past time.

Roller derby sprung from humble beginnings. The sport was an idea birthed in 1933 by Leo Seltzer, who scribbled notes on a tablecloth in Chicago's old Rickett's restaurant about a marathon-type race. Seltzer's vision embraced a track upon which men and women on wheels competed in a race of stamina and speed.

The early game did not include the "smash and crash" fierceness that most people associate with derby. Instead, it fit with the times. The worst of the Great Depression had hit the U.S. economy, and marathons of all types as a means of entertainment were cropping up. Competitions were taking over—dance marathons, ice-sitting contests—and derby was intended to be

Taking a cue from hockey, the penalty box was soon adopted into derby. (above)

Whether real or slightly dramatized, fighting became more of a mainstay in derby. (left)

another among them. The skating track was flat, and the skaters glided on wheels made out of wood to reach their goal, which was to skate continuously for almost twelve hours.

Under the name of the Transcontinental Roller Derby, Leo Seltzer debuted the game on August 12, 1935, to more than 20,000 spectators crammed into the Chicago Coliseum. Fans watched as coed teams skated 57,000 laps (roughly the distance across the United States).

With such a huge response from the public, Leo chose cities across the nation that he and his athletes could visit via bus, assemble their flat track, and let the derby loose. The track had to be set up and torn down at each new place, which took time, so the derby would stay in each location for a while, sometimes for stretches of a few weeks.

To fans, Leo's Transcontinental Roller Derby was one of many of its kind, and there was a perception that several teams were out there traveling the country. Audiences had no reason to believe that Leo's creation was the only real one of its kind; after all, there was no means of rapid communication at the time, so fans simply relied on what little they heard.

A "home team" was always featured in every city the derby visited. But in reality, it was one of Leo's teams acting as the home team, while his other team was said to be comprised of the rival players from another city. This approach added an extra air of excitement to the game—fans knew which team they wanted to cheer for, which skaters were on their side, and their hometown pride added extra incentive to go to the game.

The skaters reveled in the travel. They got to meet local officials who would make guest appearances to kick off the first game of a run. They were treated with celebrity status—granting interviews to local newspapers and parading up and down streets in their skates to drum up excitement for the games. Not only were they recruiting local fans in each city, they were also soliciting new skaters who might be interested in running away with the derby.

Participants were not only hired on for their speed or skating ability; men and women who could add entertainment value to the show via talent and personality were also signed. In addition

Women relished the opportunity to be unapologetically physical in derby. (above)

Look closely on the Bay Bomber's hip and you'll see a skull and crossbones, something you'd see in today's derby. (left)

to skating, some of the coed teams would sing or dance for money. Roller derby skaters had to know how to capture a crowd's attention and keep it. They had to have presence.

Skaters came from all walks of life. Speed skaters fled the confines of their local rinks in droves and young men and women with less than palatable home situations left at a young age with the goal of becoming self-sufficient. After all, jobs were scarce at the time, and Leo provided skaters with the rare blessings of shelter, medical care, and food.

A career as a derby skater was considered a good job during the Depression, with an impressive payoff for those days. The skaters had to be committed to the game and train hard, but they always had a roof over their heads and were guaranteed payment. For female skaters, it meant something else: the derby was America's

first real chance to see women compete on an equalized playing field. Though men and women didn't skate directly against each other, they were governed by the same rules. By many accounts, they were even paid equally, and some say women were paid more for joining, as female athletes were more scarce.

When forty-seven-year-old Josephine "Ma" Bogash joined together with her son, Buddy Bogash, to form a team, she did it in an effort to lose weight but also to win a dare from her husband and prove that not only could she become a derby skater, she could become one of the best. In her determination, she also inadvertently attracted an entirely new audience—housewives.

Women across the nation delighted in the chance to watch female athletes their own age fiercely compete the way Ma Bogash did. Leo tapped into the previously nonexistent pool of

National

ROLLER
DERBY

female fans by selling tickets at places where women were likely to frequent: grocery stores and fabric shops.

Most women simply didn't relate to football or baseball players of their time, and the other options for entertainment, such as movies, didn't provide an adequate release during such trying times. But the ladies of the era could somehow envision themselves racing across the smooth track, bent low at the knees, propelling themselves forward with force of will and each well-timed stroke of the legs.

At last, women could escape their daily doldrums and even release some pent-up aggression. The support of women no doubt helped raise roller derby to its position as a major sport in the country.

FROM SKATING TO SCUFFLING

A points system was eventually introduced to the game. The look of the game changed further when Leo Seltzer introduced the banked track. The flat track was tipped to accommodate a forty-five-degree angle, adding significant speed to the races.

Leo was a natural promoter. Not content to maintain the status quo, he quickly upped the ante and the antics on the track. Whether mandated by him or not, hip checking, body blocking, and all-out brawls entered the picture. And when skaters fell, they were required to remain on the track until medical personnel could remove them.

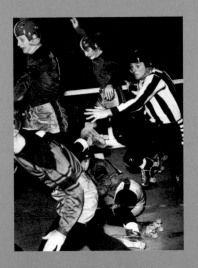

Referees called the shots deep within the pack. (above)

Put more than one skater hell-bent on victory on a track of any sort and they'll try to lap each other, get around each other, and win at all costs…even at the risk of bodily harm. Eventually, they'll collide; and collide they did. Skaters became increasingly competitive as the popularity of the sport grew, and entanglements on the track became more and more common. The fact that crowds seemed to love it when skaters stumbled or got tied up on the track did not go unnoticed.

At the prompting of famed New York sportswriter Damon Runyan, Leo decided not to discourage the full-contact aspect of the game but instead incorporate the collisions. At this turning point, roller derby was no longer just an endurance sport. Now,

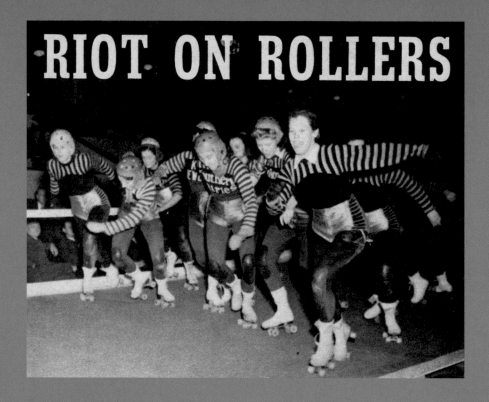

RIOT ON ROLLERS

instead of having several teams who raced each other in pairs, there would be two rival teams battling it out.

Each team had ten skaters, five of each sex. Each position had a male and female skater, for a total of four jammers and six blockers. These skaters scored a point each time they passed a member of the opposing team. Contact was completely necessary, considering that the goal of the game was to work through a mass of skaters. Players had to restrategize and play offense and defense at the same time. Leo continued to alter the rules of the game based on what the fans wanted, tweaking the rules of can and can't.

While the rules of derby altered and changed over the years, the love of the game never wavered. (above)

The traditional male/female roles occurred off the track, despite their equality come bout time. (right)

Arenas were crowded in every location where the derby was to take place. Fans became increasingly enthralled in the action, screaming and yelling until the walls of derby venues vibrated. Security guards had to escort certain skaters for fear of crazed fans lashing out. The energy only fueled the skaters to skate faster and block harder. And thus, the *real* roller derby was born.

The skaters were tough. They'd suffered through injuries—broken bones, cracked ribs, and even punctured eardrums—from the beginning. The media fed more on relaying these tales of tragedy and gossiping about the private lives of skaters than reporting the actual action of the game. Still, *sportswriters* were beginning to cover the sport.

By 1941, sponsors were offering money to help cover expenses for individual skaters and sometimes for entire teams. An overwhelming number of sensational skaters formed a total of eight solid squads, and fans responded to them all. Derby was becoming a true American mainstay.

BEHIND THE SCENES

Leo Seltzer may have founded, owned, and improved roller derby when he added a slight bank, or tilt, to the track, but the skaters kept it alive and thriving.

Skaters traveled together, stayed together in bunks, and cooked together, forming a family of sorts, bartering with each other to accomplish everything that needed to be done in their makeshift "households on the road."

While roller derby played a big part in the equalizing of the sexes, the traditional roles that marked the times were still in

*Midge "Toughie" Brasuhn,
one of derby's superstars, truly
lived up to her nickname.
(above)*

some sense maintained. Female skaters did laundry in return for
having their wheels ground by male skaters.

While spending so much time together, it was natural that
love bloomed between skaters. At first, Leo discouraged affairs
between his players, but he soon realized that it could work to
his benefit. After all, skaters understood each other and wouldn't
be convinced by civilian spouses that the derby was a ridiculous
pursuit.

Some skaters married each other and started families, all the
while remaining active in the derby. And their kids even got
into the fun. The Diaper Derby featured skaters' kids who would
have speed races at selected games for the goal of winning a
silver dollar.

THE ROLLER DERBY HALL OF FAME

Eventually, as the game became more of a spectacle, heroes and
villains alike began to emerge among the ranks. True to their ste-
reotypes, these standouts wowed crowds with their all-American
looks and style or carried on the types of feuds associated today
with pro-wrestling. Audiences grew to adore skaters not only for
their athleticism and agility but also for their character, dramatic
performances, and off-the-track antics.

There were good girls like Joanie Weston, bad girls including Ann
Calvello, and everything in between. Fans looked up to the derby
skaters and even began to mimic them, granting them idol status.

Gerry Murray hair bows surfaced in the late fifties and were
marketed as accessories "worn by the Queens of the Roller
Derby." Murray was considered one of derby's good girls. She

was heralded as a natural skater and is said to be one of the highest-scoring female skaters of her time. She captained the New York City Chiefs for a period and made derby a family affair when she married a skater and gave birth to a would-be derby skater, Mike Gammon.

Murray's rivalry with Midge "Toughie" Brasuhn is still talked about today by derby fans and skaters. Brasuhn, a Brooklyn Red

Though American born, derby caught on in Europe, here in Paris, France. (above)

Devil, is rumored to have been a feared, heavy-drinking brawler who truly gave Murray a run for her money on the rink, rivaling her natural skating ability and elevating the excitement of the games. Brasuhn was one of derby's true superstars. She once even starred on a billboard in New York sporting an oversized jersey, tousled hair, and remnants of the track's slate on her face. The tagline "Who is Toughie?" enticed fans and gave them a taste of what to expect from Brasuhn as a skater.

Murray and Brasuhn emerged respectively as the sugar and spice of derby. Together with Murray, Brasuhn helped put female athletes on the map. They pushed each other to become stronger athletes and better performers. They proved that they were just as competitive as men, and they illustrated just how committed to the game they were.

The roller derby skaters of the times prided themselves on their skating agility, speed, and athleticism, but because of the newfound performance aspect of the game and its accompanying personalities, the public was suspect. The skaters publicly and vehemently fended off critics who claimed their sport wasn't a real one. It was a catch-22. Skaters struggled to be taken seriously in the face of demands for increased antics and showmanship.

A WAR OFF THE TRACK

Derby was thriving by the time World War II hit. Leo Seltzer had assembled a vast army of his own, and audience response had never been higher. But all of that was halted, albeit temporarily, when most of his male skaters were drafted.

Leo weathered the storm by taking the two remaining teams he managed to hold together on a national tour. He kept the

operation afloat, and when the war ended, most of his players returned to derby. Leo had his skaters back, but it was up to him to build the derby back up to the status it had achieved before the war.

Determined to do just that, Leo set out to ensure that television took note of his sport. In a departure from the radio and newspaper efforts he traditionally embraced, Leo courted several television stations to no avail. Until, on November 29, 1948, the first televised roller derby game was broadcast live from New York. It was the first of seventeen games to be played in the 69th Regiment Armory.

The telecast raised awareness of the sport to such an extent that Leo was up that night taking reservations for future games instead of sleeping. After that, crowds swelled to the point where the police were called in to restore order and the armory was at last filled to capacity.

It had taken fifteen years to get roller derby to the point where Leo Seltzer truly intended it to be, and he had the American public right where he wanted them—hooked on America's greatest sport. And when the public wants something, so does the media; the derby made headlines and was featured in national magazine spots, and the tables were turned when the networks began courting Leo instead of the other way around.

With the Big Apple conquered, it was time for Leo to truly take his operation national. The National Roller Derby League was created and, under it, several clubs operated: New York Chiefs, Brooklyn Red Devils, Jersey Jolters, Philadelphia Panthers, Chicago Westerners, and Washington (D.C.) Jets. All but the Red Devils actually skated in their respective locales. Fake home teams were no longer forced to materialize; now the country had the real deal.

The zenith of the game (up until this point) took hold in June 1949 when Madison Square Garden saw 55,000 tickets sell for a five-day world series. Derby games were being broadcast sometimes three times a week, all with an increase in ticket prices.

This all took a toll on the skaters. As a condition of Leo's television contract, the skaters were allowed no off-season. Through the next three years, derby was televised live, fifty-two weeks a year.

Roller derby had hit the prime time. Literally.

2 ROLLER DERBY MEETS ROLLERJAM

Television ushered in a whole new level of fame for roller derby. It seemed to have finally infiltrated popular culture, and, accordingly, Leo Seltzer left the television station he originally contracted with in search of bigger and better ratings. But all the while, Leo was unwittingly fighting a battle he didn't see coming. Television was actually negating the need for derby, changing the face of entertainment in America.

With more choices for how to spend their leisure time, fans began questioning the legitimacy of the sport and no longer embraced the on-track antics that once helped make the sport popular. Television executives responded in kind. The other stations Leo pursued turned their backs on derby.

Yet Leo persevered. He believed, with or without television, there was life for the sport. For the sake of his skaters, who had dedicated lifetimes to perfecting their craft, it was a good thing Leo did. Most roller derby skaters knew no other life and were ill equipped, if equipped at all, to hang up their wheels and adopt white-collar jobs.

Leo made the most of his old-school promotion techniques; he headed back to newspaper and radio and continued to draw crowds to his live games. But without television backing and due to oversaturation, the sport floundered on home territory. Thus, Leo Seltzer took his game to Europe, skating in England, France, and Spain.

Back in the states in 1953, despite Leo's prior belief that derby could only thrive with a strong presence in New York, the derby slowly headed out West. Leo began considering smaller productions and alternative ways to feature derby, at least in spirit. But, as a means for financial survival for him and his family, he began pursuing an alternate career and, ultimately, prepared for retirement. Derby, however, didn't die, and remained in the family.

THE BUSINESS OF ROLLER DERBY

Leo's son Jerry assumed control of what was left of the venture and moved it to northern California, getting things rolling again. Though the sport and rules remained largely the same, the transition from old Seltzer to young Seltzer was the first movement of what now seems to be a natural ebb and flow of the sport. Different views of what's important—sport or packaging—almost always have an unwitting effect on the game.

Leo had poured himself heart and soul into the game and his skaters; Jerry took a more distant approach, treating derby like the money-making venture it was. Both Seltzers were admired and trusted leaders with the same goal of keeping derby afloat, yet both embraced very different approaches to reaching it.

Famed sports announcer Dick Lane stands between the fists of Raquel Welch and Patti "Moo Moo" Cavin in Kansas City Bomber. (above)

Skaters stuck in the middle struggled with their own value sets. They too hoped to keep roller derby, their lifeblood, alive, yet wondered whether they would be better off staying true to the sport or adopting the theatrical antics that seemed to draw the crowds.

Skaters knew how to showboat and stand out to the crowd, but they still trained harder than ever and visibly took offense to allusions that derby was anything other than a true sport. Their laundry list of injuries was proof positive that the hazards of the game were indeed real. As has been the case in most of the sport's past and present, the skaters ultimately chose to include both aspects of sport and theatrics in the game.

Small stations aired tapes of bouts, which seemed to do well. Jerry used the medium differently than his father had, manipulating it into a true marketing tool. Jerry aired only portions of bouts, forcing viewers who wanted in on all of the action to buy tickets to a live game. Television was reduced to mercly a hook.

The 1960s ushered in even more prosperity for roller derby. Two new roller derby operations popped up on the West Coast and broke up the monopoly the Seltzers had enjoyed for so long. Los Angeles played home to the LA Braves, San Francisco's home team was the Bay Bombers, and Portland/Seattle/Spokane called the Westerners their home team.

Even Hollywood took note of the game. Mickey Rooney starred in *The Fireball,* and Raquel Welch took to the screen as a roller babe in *Kansas City Bomber. Rollerball* with James Caan also hit the red carpet.

ROLLER DERBY®

NUMBER 7   OFFICIAL PROGRAM

35c   35c

INTERNATIONAL LEAGUE

Roller derby eventually began skating bouts against Roller Games, a Southern California rival that featured a televised version of the sport promoting more outlandish theatrics and stunts than roller derby skaters were used to. The different approaches to the game didn't always mesh. Roller derby skaters resented that their athleticism was expected to take a backseat during Roller Games matches.

AND THAT'S THE JAM

Roller derby went nationwide with teams defined by and implanted in different regions of the nation. A season consisted of 120 games per team, and home games were played in local

As with all sports, there's always the opportunity to make money through marketing; here derby skates are the name of the game. (below)

arenas. The gas crisis in the early 1970s, however, made travel impossible, and the Seltzer-owned roller derby organization held its last game on December 7, 1973, in Binghamton, New York.

Those left standing pointed toward different reasons for its end. Some blamed ticket fiascos and venue management snafus, which both caused great upheaval before the last game was played. There were also the issues of skater injuries, illnesses, and moves to competitive derby organizations; some skaters even believed Jerry's divorce played a part in the end.

Whatever the cause, Jerry Seltzer, the man who had straddled his father's Transcontinental Roller Derby and his own business of the sport, announced its end to the heart of the sport, the skaters. He confirmed to the stunned and now out-of-work group that the homegrown business presided over by generations of his family was over. Fans, skaters, and promoters alike would have to live with only memories of the game.

Promoters afterward tried to breathe new life into the game, including an effort in cooperation with ESPN, but all efforts met with limited success, if any. The most outrageous revival attempt is credited to *RollerGames*, which featured a figure eight-shaped track that was heavily banked and encumbered skaters along the way with obstacles. To break ties, skaters raced around an alligator pit located in the middle of the track for five consecutive laps. The loser was thrown into the alligator pit. A half season was all the airwaves ever saw before *RollerGames* was cancelled due to a waning audience, financial troubles among its main production company, and poor production value.

A REVIVAL FOR THE MILLENNIUM

The late 1990s appeared to provide fertile ground for yet again reviving derby. Pro wrestling had primed the American psyche for a dose of choreographed violence, inline skating was more popular than ever, and the impending millennium delivered an air of nostalgia.

Heartfelt tributes to the fallen Joanie Weston, roller derby's "Golden Girl," who passed away in 1997, also contributed to the revival. Plus, minimal research uncovered fans and skaters alike who were keeping the sport alive, even if only in their memories. Among them was Jerry Seltzer.

Initially reluctant to again get involved in the roller coaster of a sport that formed his family's backbone, Jerry eventually took the reigns as head of the new World Skating League (WSL). He teamed with The Nashville Network (TNN), who provided ample enthusiasm, not to mention financial backing, for the vision of reviving roller derby. Thus, *RollerJam* was born.

Derby was back, with a bridge between old and new. But Jerry wasn't *RollerJam*'s link to the past. In fact, the rules and object of the game were slated to stay largely the same but would be super-charged for the new millennium, featuring skaters in form-fitting uniforms on inline skates playing on a bigger, faster track. Once again, the sport strived to straddle the fine line between pure athleticism and good old-fashioned entertainment.

By the 1970s, the great Joanie Weston had been on the derby circuit for twenty years, and still going strong. (left)

RollerJam premiered in January 1999, this time the product of the South, seemingly no longer at the mercy of the fickle entertainment fans who lined both coasts. Jerry was poised to use his

Demon of the Derby. Villainess of Roller Derby. The Lovable Lioness. Banana Nose. Roller Derby Queen. Meanest Mama on Skates.

Ann Calvello went by many names throughout her career as a standout star of the banked track. She was the skater fans loved to hate. The one who bucked the conventional mores of her time in favor of yelling, kicking, screaming, and cursing her way to infamy.

Calvello skated for the bad guys, happily distinguishing herself from the more wholesome personas of her time. With her tanned body resplendent with tattoos and piercings, and hair spray painted the color of the day, it wasn't hard for Calvello to stand out. From the beginning, as it was in the end, she was different, she had presence. And no one could deny the sheer force of her athletic ability.

At only eighteen, Calvello attended a roller derby bout, heard that there were open spots for skaters, and ran off to travel with the banked track. She was a tomboy at heart, and the fact that derby offered an equal playing field for men and women wasn't lost on Calvello.

During the course of her long and colorful career, which spanned seven decades, Calvello played for the love of her sport. She adapted to the game's many incarnations, making comebacks here and there, and even appearing as the guest of honor at a 2005 bout. A documentary about her life, entitled *Demon of the Derby*, has made Calvello a sort of cult hero.

Even as a retired skater employed as a grocery bagger, Calvello could trump stories from any skater alive. But after overcoming brain cancer twice, Calvello lost her life to liver cancer. Look for a common thread

among the derby of past, present, and future and you'll find Calvello. She remains the patron saint of all skaters who take to the track in search of glory, a fast game, and a good time.

PENALTY BOX

business savvy and television experience once again to cater to the network's stereotype of Southern NASCAR-loving viewers and take advantage of the fact that roller derby largely appealed to viewers who were turned off by the big-money, big-time athletes of their day.

Yet, finding skaters and even securing fans proved a challenge for Jerry and the network executives. Most of the players eligible to skate and the fans who comprised television's most desirable demographic were simply too young to really remember the game.

So, how *do* you find athletes who can play a game that's been dead for twenty-five years? You put out casting calls, of course. Jerry beckoned Hollywood-style to speed skaters, roller hockey players, extreme sports enthusiasts, and even American Gladiators and creamed-corn wrestlers. Respondents were predominantly speed skaters, but when ultimately put through the paces, often by true-blue, old-school roller derby players, not everyone passed the test. Speed skaters weren't used to fighting and taking hits while on wheels, a requirement for *RollerJam* players.

Those athletes who could take on the job traveled to the home of *RollerJam*, Universal Studios Florida in Orlando. The studio played host to *RollerJam*'s six teams: New York Enforcers, Florida Sundogs, California Quakes, Nevada High Rollers, Texas Twisters, and Illinois Inferno. *RollerJam*'s debut game had more than 2.9 million viewers and was the most-watched cable show during its time period among males ages twelve to thirty-four.

The Enforcers played the role of the heavies in what would be one of the world's first reality shows mixed with sport. They were modeled to be true byproducts of the city from which

RollerJam *had concocted plots, but the blows were painfully real. (right)*

Derby Meets RollerJam

their namesake hailed: They were aggressive, and the members of the men's starting line up were called the "Five Boroughs." They represented the bad guys, dressed completely in black, and disregarded the rules of play in favor of all-out physical contact.

As it was in the past, skaters showed individual personality and style. One of the Enforcers' male starters, Brian Gamble, listed playing with knives as his chief hobby. The women were portrayed as loud, vocal, and opinionated, and were led by a bodybuilder known as "The Minister of Pain."

In true television fashion, where there are bad guys (and girls), you must have a goody two-shoes to offset them. And so the Sundogs team was born. Sundog players claimed that they were fit only to play the game and didn't take personal vengeance out on the track. They played by the rules.

RollerJam was a true Hollywood-style production. It marketed rivalries, friendships, and love affairs to drama-hungry sports fans. The competition was manipulated and storylines concocted, though the athletes carrying them out had no stunt doubles— the pain and force involved in playing their "characters" was 100 percent real. On the track, there was simply no way to predict and choreograph each skater's move or reaction to a blow. Once again, the athletes' injuries proved the action was legitimate. Skaters counted cracked vertebrae, broken arms, broken noses, blown out MCLs, cuts, and bruises among the war wounds. The complete package promised an engaging battle.

Toward the end of its second-year stretch, *RollerJam*'s ratings began to dwindle. In an effort to keep it afloat, producers resorted to drastic and desperate changes, including evening-gown battles. Catfights took precedence over competition, thus disrupting the delicate balance of sport and color that had previously kept the sport alive. It translated into poor taste rather than an increase in viewers, proving that while people may be drawn to drama and storylines, they want to see real athleticism.

Unable to deliver, TNN dropped *RollerJam* with unaired episodes left in the waiting pool, including one that would reunite Ann Calvello with the track. The last episode of *RollerJam* appeared on January 19, 2001.

A final statement from *RollerJam* on January 27, 2001, read: *We've witnessed two years of smashes, crashes, thrills, and spills in the* RollerJam *arena. Dozens of athletes traveled from around the country to take part in this revived sport and test their skills on the banked track. Now sadly the games are over. Hopefully everyone involved—from the skaters to the crew behind the scenes to the fans in the stands—will walk away (or skate away) with fond memories of this experience.* RollerJam *opened up a new chapter in roller derby history, updating the sport for a new generation. Inline skates, high-flying stunts, and youthful athletes gave traditional roller derby fans something to talk about and introduced the sport to new fans who had never experienced roller derby in their lives.*

Whatever the opinion of *RollerJam* at the time of its demise, it holds firmly to its place as having an important impact on roller derby's revival. It may not have mimicked the old-school game enough for die-hard fans, but it settled into its own niche and upheld the tradition of hard working, dedicated skaters.

Many of the skaters today recall watching RollerJam, *not realizing the impact it would have on their future. (right)*

And, thankfully, this wasn't the end for derby.

3

FROM DUST TO DERBY

Ask any modern-day roller girl where the heart of derby lies today and she'll no doubt tell you Austin, Texas. It's hot, it's humid, it's known for being weird, and it's roller girl central.

It wasn't always. Austin became the birthplace of the derby revival in 2000, when a few girls from the city were invited to join in a circus-infused, punk-rock-themed version of the game that focused more on staged antics then athleticism. That formula had already been proven a failure and almost killed the sport again when the man heading up the production left the idea, the sport, and the skaters behind. Unconvinced it should all go with him, the skaters formed Bad Girl Good Woman (BGGW) Productions. The sports and entertainment group was designed to enable them to call the shots in business and in skating.

This time, the organizers added a twist to the sport—no men allowed. Sexy uniforms, skater alter egos, and new-school rules combined with unparalleled athleticism and fearlessness. The new breed of roller derby girls all proved that you *can* bring something back. Do it differently, put a fresh spin on it, and fans will respond. In July 2002, the first public bout put on by the BGGW squad attracted about 600 enthusiasts, new and old, to Playland Skate Center.

ROLLER DERBY
LIVES

SATURDAY MAY 6 · BRONX GRIDLOCK vs. MANHATTAN MAYHEM

FRIDAY JUNE 2 · QUEENS OF PAIN vs. BROOKLYN BOMBSHELLS

THE SCHWARTZ ATHLETIC CENTER, BROOKLYN CAMPUS OF LONG ISLAND UNIVERSITY, 1 UNIVERSITY PLAZA
B, M, Q or R TO DEKALB AVENUE; 2/3, 4/5 TO NEVINS STREET
DOORS OPEN AT 7:30 TIX: $12.50 ADVANCE, $15 AT DOOR

Roller derby bouts are full-scale productions. While the emphasis at practice is always about training, bout time provides roller girls with the chance to amp-up their alter egos. (left)

Austin, Texas, is known as the birthplace of derby's revival. (right)

Disputes over the management of the league ultimately divided the girls, some of them leaving to form Texas Rollergirls, a flat-track league. The remaining BGGW skaters purchased an original banked track and changed their name to Texas Roller Derby Lonestar Rollergirls. The two leagues still regularly bout to sold-out crowds.

Arizona Roller Derby followed the Texas Rollergirls and was the next flat-track league on the docket to be established. Shortly

ROLL ON, MAMA

Most roller girls balance life, work, and relationships with the all-encompassing sport that is roller derby. But so many, miraculously, also somehow still manage to make motherhood their number one priority. Who knew derby and parenting complemented each other so well!

Michelle "8 Track" Bowlin, a thirty-eight-year-old mom and Texas Rollergirl, says being a roller derby skater has lent a lot to her life as a mom of six kids. "Roller derby has had a huge effect on me as a mother of daughters. They get living, breathing proof that you do not have to fit any image

you see in a magazine to be smart, sexy, or athletic."

And perhaps being a mother has helped 8 Track deal with the ups and downs of being intimately involved in a roller derby league. "If you're a managing member of the league, it can feel just like having sixty daughters," Bowlin says in a tongue-in-cheek tone. "Just like children, roller girls are strong willed and independent. They also like to play 'dress up' just like kids. Buckin' the system and authority is another thing we have in common with kids." Bowlin's husband, whose own career includes cage fighting, understands the demands placed on her by the sport she loves so much and is able to pitch in at home so 8 Track can pursue her own dreams.

Melanee "Darth Hater" Galoardi of the Philly Rollergirls is also blessed with an understanding husband, despite the fact that she and her equally-busy mate are able to spend only two nights together a week. Her husband stays home with the kids many nights so that she can attend practice. "He's really great about it. He's *never* said that I spend too much time on derby…that would be one fight that he would not win!"

The kids get in on the action every now and then, too. Most every league's practice will find kids on the sidelines watching intently as their moms block and jam through a pack of other women on wheels. And the children oftentimes have to pitch in at bouts and meetings. The skaters eventually form their extended family, and what kid couldn't use a few dozen aunties from amazingly diverse walks of life?

The youngest member of the TXRD Lonestar Rollergirls, pictured with her skating mama Cha Cha, cheers the Putas del Fuego on at bouts. (above)

Kids are a mainstay at most bouts. In fact, plenty of leagues around the nation encourage their attendance with discounted, or even free, tickets. (left)

thereafter, Tucson Roller Derby hit the circuit, and history was made in November 2004 when all three played the first inter-league games.

The well-kept secret didn't remain landlocked—or under-ground—for long. Media attention and plain old good market-ing skills on the part of the skaters ensured that word spread. Nostalgia for quad-style skates, a lack of aggressive sports for women, and a new and viable approach to finding like-minded ladies prompted girls as far away as the Cayman Islands to reach out to the leagues already in play and find out how to bring roller derby to their parts of the world.

No longer a U.S.-only sport, derby has spread worldwide. (left)

Derby dames are ever mindful of the delicate balance between sport and spectacle. A lot of preparation is dedicated to giving the audience a show that stimulates all their senses. (right)

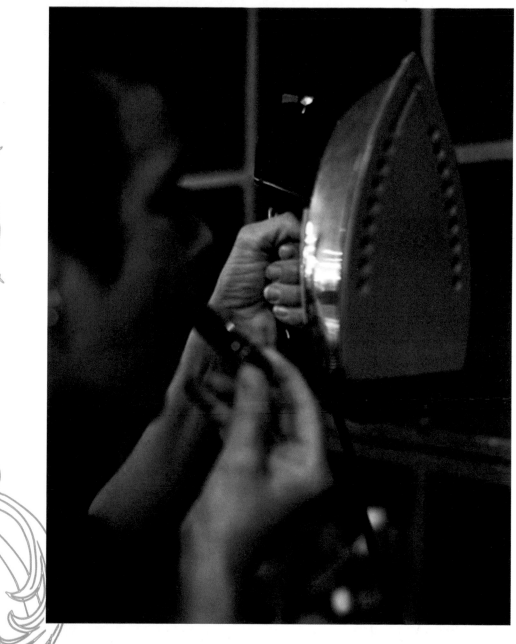

SISTERS ARE DOIN' IT

FOR THEMSELVES

The female skaters, with their fishnet stockings, quad skates, and punk-rock soundtrack, aren't just reviving roller derby, they're reinventing it. While banked tracks are still making noise, the flat-track ideal has enabled leagues to get off the ground quickly, without the need for financial backing to purchase a track and pay for a locale to store it. Flat tracks can be marked off with rope lights, duct tape, or even cones. No big investment required.

In the middle of all of the bout mayhem, roller girls have to be able to retreat inside their heads, plan their next move, and evaluate the competition. After all, the next jam is only minutes away. (above)

To lighten the load, however, leagues of all kinds sign sponsors, focusing on forming mutually beneficial relationships with local businesses and women-run organizations. The days of skater contracts and paychecks are gone; all money is funneled back into the leagues and used for travel funds, paying for practice space, purchasing merchandise, and even subsidizing the cost of injuries. With no financial payoff, many on the outskirts wonder why derby girls do it. Take a sampling of roller girls across the nation and you'll get different answers, but one common denominator will keep popping up: roller derby is fun as hell.

Surely the old-school queens of roller derby would approve. After all, this go-around the skaters themselves are the driving force behind what happens on the track *and* off. In addition to skating upward of three to four days a week, skaters assume second, unpaid jobs as public relations directors, volunteer wranglers, art directors, sponsorships chairs, and committee

Flat tracks can be set up anywhere there's a large enough level surface— abandoned airport hangers, historic theaters, etc. (below)

ALL IN THE FAMILY

For Colleen "Crackerjack" Bell, roller derby runs in the family. Bell's sister Lucille Brawl skates for the Texas Rollergirls' Hotrod Honeys, and, not content to sit on the sidelines while her younger sibling took to the track, Bell formed the Mad Rollin' Dolls of Madison, Wisconsin.

"I saw the Texas Rollergirls play and wanted to kick their asses," Bell says. "I started having visions of some scary Mad Max-themed team rolling up in a bus and rolling in to Playland and kickin' the snot out of the Hotrod Honeys."

Today, Bell is captain of her league's travel team, the Dairyland Dolls, and also skates for the home team, the Reservoir Dolls.

The most frustrating part of derby for Bell is the meetings. But the fun outweighs the labor of business. She's quick on the draw to explain what it is about derby that gets her motor running: "The game, the girls, turning left, going fast, hitting people, the fans, the after parties, the panties."

heads responsible for ensuring that leagues hold a dominant presence coast-to-coast.

Don't be fooled by the sexy uniforms, playful attitudes, and *nomes de guerre*. Roller derby is serious business. As their own She-E-Os, managing partners, and boards of directors, these women advocate a "for the skater, by the skater" business ethic that translates into full-scale bouts. Roller derby has always been more than a sport.

HELL ON (ALBEIT FLASHY) WHEELS

The current sport is rooted in derby years past but has been updated with an edgier attitude and the addition of a few modern touches such as tattooed team members, cheeky uniforms, and risqué penalties, thus creating a crowd-pleasing, fierce competition that's rougher and tougher than ever.

Uncensored yet dignified, bouts are a completely unique form of entertainment. Picture disco lights, live bands, DJs, mascots, and women in full protective gear racing at high speed, occasionally breaking to fight. Bouts also provide a nod to more traditional sports—there are referees, and often the national anthem is sung. Roller girls are constantly conscious of the divine balance between sport and show.

"The inherent nature of the sport is very showy," Mishel "Violet Temper" Cobb of the Philly Rollergirls points out. "Skating is something that will always captivate audiences and generate enthusiasm. But our names and uniforms and themes are also very creative, which is where athleticism and performance

Roller girls show their unique style from head to toe. Even protective gear isn't safe from personal expression! (left)

A SKATER
BY ANY OTHER NAME

By day, roller girls may seem to be everyday people going by everyday names. But come practice time, their personas, as well as their names, change. Jen becomes Hydra, Tessa becomes Alma Bichess, and Shannon becomes Rosie Bloodbath. Juanna Rumbel, Sharon Needles, Roxy Balboa, and Dinah-Mite also take to the track.

Derby names are a badge of honor. In fact, most leagues require a training period before roller girls can be put through their paces, earn their places in the league, and, consequently, claim their derby names.

Derby names don't come easily. The time leading up to the choice is filled with much brainstorming and even research. Friends, family, fellow derby girls, and even coworkers get involved in the hunt. Many aspects of a derby girl's life are taken into account.

Ji Lee, who skates for the Minnesota RollerGirls, came up with about twenty different names before settling on the moniker Ji Spot. The twenty-six-year-old graphic designer by day explains, "One day, fellow skater Sayonara Pussy contacted me and told me that I should use my real name and yet get creative at the same time. That's how 'Ji Spot' was born. It's flirty, cheerful, yet tough in the rink. You can't go wrong with that."

Some skaters want a derby name that is threatening, while others desire witty and cute. Some names are born of tributes, while others have sentimental meaning or even reflect a skater's personal obsession or profession. Others encompass it all.

"First, I'm a hydrologist by profession, so 'Hydra' was the feminine short-name for my job title," says Jen "Hydra" Wilson, who skates for the Texas Rollergirls' Hotrod Honeys. "Second, a hydra is an ancient mythological creature that lived in the bogs. It had nine heads. If you cut one head off, two would grow back in its place, and they would be twice as mean!"

Once a derby name is born, roller girls cross-check a master roster of all skater names to make sure that it or something close to it hasn't already been claimed. While most skater names aren't copyrighted, derby etiquette dictates that monikers not be duplicated and those already taken are honored.

As time goes on and leagues develop, derby girls often come to know each other only by their aliases; birth names become secondary.

mingle. But if we were just skating, we'd call ourselves Lisa or Jen or Mary."

Don't be fooled, however, into thinking the competition is staged. When the whistle blows, the outcome is anyone's guess, and the falls and spills are the real deal. Nothing is predetermined in derby, but there are rules. Hip, shoulder, and full-body checking are fully legal. Skaters do what it takes to get their jammer—the point-scoring skater—through the pack of opposing blockers. Strategy, fierce competition, and trademark moves are paramount to derby girls.

THE JAM OF TODAY

In Seattle, there are plenty of passionate derby-fan converts raising the roof about the religion of roller derby. (above left)

The LA Derby Dolls train and prepare for bouts on a banked, oval track. (below left)

It's not easy finding venues affordable and large enough to semi-permanently house a banked track. The skaters of the LA Derby Dolls and TXRD Lonestar Rollergirls have both worked hard to secure appropriate practice and bouting venues for their active leagues.

And flat-track leagues pound the pavement just as hard, scouring their neighborhoods to find level flooring, a space unencumbered by poles, and enough floor room to mark off a track. Then there's the matter of convincing venue owners that fans should

Each roller derby league has its own unique team theme, yet, while conforming to the theme, roller girls frequently put their own touches on their uniforms. (left)

sit directly in harm's way, close enough to the track that out-of-bounds skaters frequently land in their laps.

Out of necessity, leagues have gotten creative in sizing up locales, including not only traditional roller skating rinks but also old theaters, inline hockey venues, outdoor skateboarding parks, abandoned airline hangars, warehouses, ballrooms, and even bars and clubs. And somehow, they're finding kismet with the location owners who want a piece of the nation's hottest new comeback.

Whatever the venue, crowds line up early to get the best seats. For banked-track viewers, this means staggered bleachers positioned for a view of the track, a spot where they can see each skater hopping over the railing to hit the Masonite or, during the game, being flipped over the track by a rival. In the case of flat-track bouts, the floor space directly next to the track is prime real estate. There the only thing separating them from the skaters is some flooring and caution tape.

Fans keep a firm grip on their beer. Emcees train fans precariously close to the boundaries of the track how to hoist their beer and save their brew from skaters who fall into the crowd. "Beers, broads, and bruises are what we're here for," Heather "Betsy Blackheart" Dalton, emcee for Denver's Rocky Mountain Rollergirls, explains before each bout. "And having your beer spilled by a broad on wheels is very, very good luck." *That* is how derby legend is born.

Whichever your preferred type of play—new or old, banked or flat—bouts of all types have something in common: fan energy. Current players as well as those who skated decades ago attribute some of their best bouts to fans, more specifically the crowd

WOMEN'S FLAT TRACK DERBY ASSOCIATION

Basketball has the NBA, hockey the NHL, and today's badass roller derby queens of the flat track have the Women's Flat Track Derby Association (WFTDA). While not (yet) a professional sports organization, the WFTDA is well on its way.

At the first sign that the roller derby revival would catch on nationwide, the first few league founders joined together to share information and create a unified structure that would form the foundation of all-female flat-track roller derby. In 2004, as other leagues began to form and were added to the forum, the WFTDA was created. Since then, the association has worked to standardize and continually revise a set of rules for flat-track interleague play, and is adopting a ranking-and-standard skill-level policy.

Representatives from member leagues meet periodically to reaffirm their intentions to foster new leagues and the legitimacy of the sport. They also conquer such tasks as standardizing a set of rules, setting seasons, and determining guidelines for the national and international athletic competitions of member leagues.

The organization operates on a "by the skaters, for the skaters" work ethic, much like the one upon which its members' leagues are built. Female skaters make up the vast majority of member league management and, consequently, of the association. All member leagues are heard when it comes to decision making and voting, and, in return, member leagues agree to comply with the WFTDA governing body's policies.

The earliest fruits of the WFTDA's potentials were realized in February 2006, when the Tucson Roller Derby organized and hosted the Dust Devil Tournament, the first-ever, groundbreaking interleague tournament of its kind. WFTDA member leagues across the nation assembled the best of the best to go up against each other, determined to take home the national title of 2006 Dust Devil Champion. Incidentally, the Texas Rollergirls of Austin took home the crown.

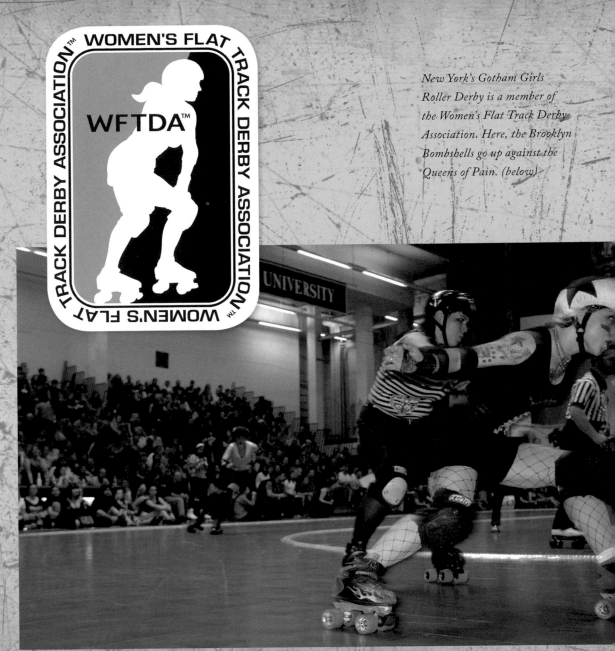

New York's Gotham Girls Roller Derby is a member of the Women's Flat Track Derby Association. Here, the Brooklyn Bombshells go up against the Queens of Pain. (below)

response, which fuels them and keeps them going well into the last minutes of the final period.

Mascots, referees, and a penalty princess all make appearances, and a DJ is often on hand to set the skating to an appropriate beat. Once the crowds, assisted by the emcee and oftentimes by a full bar, are worked into a frenzy, skaters from rival teams make their debut, skating a lap around the track while being introduced by their derby names—Alma Bichess, Cha Cha, Basket Casey, Crazy Duke, La Muerta, Fisti Cuffs, Dottie Karate. Their monikers are an indicator of what's to come, and, judging by the fans' reactions, they know it.

BOUT TIME

Bouts consist of anywhere from two to three periods for flat track and four periods for banked. Periods last between eight and twelve minutes, depending on the style of play and league rules. Likewise, periods are split up into sixty-second (banked track) or two-minute (flat track) jams. Each jam kicks off with five members from each team on the track. Four members from each team—three blockers led by one pivot, who sets the pace and acts as the last line of defense—start in a pack. The jammers, who score points for each team, bring up the rear.

In a nutshell, as a blocker or pivot, the goal is to use your body to get the other team members out of the way of your jammer. Get the jammer through or past the pack and she scores points on the opposing team members left behind. But there's also the issue of blocking the other team's jammer while you're at it. The jammer's responsibility: Get through the pack and do it in bounds. Don't let anyone get in the way.

Roller girls never know which way a bout will go or what their opponents have in store for them until they hit the track. Strategizing has to occur on the fly, in between jams, and during half times and time outs. (right)

It all translates into action so intense that some leagues charge up to seven referees with keeping the peace and the score. Girls use each other to create a wall the opposing jammer can do little but plow into at full speed. Distracted blockers, their heads on a swivel, are knocked unsuspectingly into the infield or even into their own teammates. Jammers can even get into the mix, taking one another out early in a jam to lessen the pressure of catching the pack.

All-out brawls are the only thing known to stop the skating. Girls explode into fisticuffs, pounding on each other before screaming crowds. And there's only so much hitting, bumping, and blocking the sport's more colorful characters will take before they retaliate—sometimes even illegally, making the split-second decision that a fight is worth the penalty. Sidelined skaters have been known to storm the track, sink their teeth into referees' ankles, and try to steal the spotlight from emcees.

Roller girls take advantage of the rare opportunity to show that they can give it as well as they can take it. "Women rarely have an outlet to be physically aggressive and unapologetically competitive but remain friends," says Rebekah "Ivana Clobber" Allen, who skates for the Boston Derby Dames.

The strict and precise set of rules governing the game means there's also punishment for breaking or just plain ignoring them. Derby zebras are made, not born, and are vital to the game both in terms of sport and in show. Windy City Rollers' Marc "Chicago Ace" Stern keeps the peace at Chicago's main alterna-attraction and once disqualified both teams when they stormed the track during a bout. The final score: 0-0.

Penalties are standard fare at any bout, but how they are doled out is at the league's discretion. For some leagues, punishment equals time in a penalty box, during which the offending skater's team must play short. Other leagues force skaters to spin a wheel of misfortune presided over by a penalty princess or knock on the doors of discipline. Generally, the biggest offenders are rounded up and given the chance to earn a point back for their team via penalty games.

It can't be stated enough that derby girls do it all; some even sing the national anthem before a bout. (left)

In Las Vegas, the Sin City Rollergirls' penalty games entail two skaters squaring off in a hardcore arm-wrestling match. More intricate penalty games include Fat Guy Races, during which two oversized men sit in wheelchairs and are propelled around the track by skaters in a race to the finish. Spank Alley is also a popular punishment—a ref drags a skater past fans who get to take a shot at her.

Peanalties aside, skaters get only a few brief opportunities to catch their collective breath by way of time-outs and short breaks between periods. The only real chance to regroup and, in the case of the team lagging behind, restrategize comes during halftime, when the crowd is engulfed in derby-inspired sideshows. Think local bands, buskers, bag pipers, belly dancers, and burlesque girls. The acts not only complement the spirit in which derby is played, they keep an already energized crowd on its toes, preparing them for the bout's final outcome.

PARTY'S OVER; PARTY BEGINS

When the bout is over, you'll see skaters from both teams lapping the track. Full-fledged ass kickers turn back into sisters, their bodies pushed to the limits, thresholds for a good time surpassed. At least until the afterparty.

What would all that hard work be for without a celebration? Whether the girls invite fans back to their favorite bars for "Bitch Slap" or "Black and Blue" shots or host a private party at a local club, fans are just as happy to see them off their

wheels, dissecting the evening's best plays and congratulating each other on their respective fishnet burns, assorted scrapes, bruises, and occasional stitches.

Roller girls play to skate, skate to win, and toast it all regardless of what happens. There's always the next bout.

Battles for domination of the banked track go on in Austin and Los Angeles. (below)

ROLLING THUNDER

Derby dames are not just the bad girls who used to smoke in the high school bathroom; they're also the ones who ratted them out. An image of what makes a derby girl has been put forth to fans, an image resplendent with a neo-punk aesthetic. Fans may attend bouts expecting to see a certain type of girl—with piercings, multi-colored hair, and whatever other physical characteristics they've come to associate with "tough." But the reality doesn't necessarily fit the stereotype. With derby, what you see isn't always what you get.

While derby dames may share shoulder aches and swollen ankles, there is no way to fit them all in one box. In reality, you're as likely to find quiet-minded students, stay-at-home moms, and corporate nine-to-fivers storming tracks around the nation as you are to see the skaters with forearms full of ink. A variety of women respond to the siren song of derby—one that lures them into a world where they can sweat, skate, and scuffle into the hearts of fans around the world…that, and they *do* get to wear cute uniforms.

Chances are, whatever skaters do during the day, they'll be tasked to put those skills to work for their roller derby league.

A variety of roles is needed to keep the business side of things running and thriving, and the girls must be up to the challenge.

With derby being such a unique sport and business endeavor, it's hard pressed to mirror any other business model. There is no handbook for creating a successful league, yet women around the nation are doing it, doing it well, and proving that the corporate world of business isn't the only entity out there. Skaters take great pride in the fact that leagues are not traditional top-down organizations. Most employ some form of democratic ruling system and make it work to their advantage. Roller girls spend as much time on off-the-rink business as they do practicing, but it's a way of doing business that works.

Roller derby is as real a sport as it gets, and training has nothing to do with choreographed moves. It instead encompasses agility, stretching, strength, and speed. (below)

While Ann Calvello was the original "Demon of the Derby," plenty of skaters today uphold the tradition she started: one of mixing fast, hard play with arresting appearances and self expression. (right)

"Real life," as roller girls often refer to time spent during the day on activities other than derby, is important, but derby is a really close second. Every girl in a league is expected to pull her weight. For the privilege of skating, maintaining a place on a team, and calling herself a warrior on eight wheels, she in return is responsible for a portion, however big or small, of the upkeep of the league.

It's many a woman's dream: the chance to be unapologetically sexy and at the same time athletic, tough, fearless, and business-minded; the opportunity to show society that they are complex, multi-faceted, multi-layered women with skills and interests beyond the home and career.

SKATING IN THE SHADOWS

OF LEGENDS

The tradition of arresting appearances and behavior is nothing new to derby. With roots planted in 1948, Ann "Banana Nose" Calvello, also know as the original and only "Demon of the Derby," was a crowd and media darling. Calvello earned her skate name thanks to several broken noses suffered during bouts.

Ann Calvello was always more than an athlete; she was a rebel and infamously known for it. She bucked every conventional norm about what it meant to be a female athlete, which was quite a feat, considering the social norms of her day. Trading the confines of being ladylike for an aggressive style of play, Calvello adopted temper-induced antics and rivalries on the track. And as far as looks, she was spray painting her hair purple and flashing tattoos on the banked track long before today's skaters were even born.

Roller girls today idolize her as well as relate to her, which keeps her memory alive and bouting. In July 2005, Ann Calvello united the past with the present when she stood as the guest of honor for the women of TXRD Lonestar Rollergirls, witnessing the Holy Rollers and the Rhinestone Cowgirls doing battle for the Calvello Cup.

Off the rink, Calvello remained true to form and was vocal in support of the long-term health and future of roller derby. She counseled leagues across the country about how teamwork and a commitment to skating must be paramount to succeed in derby. Everything else, including looks, is secondary.

SNAPSHOT OF A DERBY GIRL

Michela "Dahmernatrix" Dai Zovi was initially drawn to derby simply because of the kitsch factor. "I wasn't sure what to think at first, but then I saw a picture of a girl wearing go-go boots with skates mounted onto them and I was hooked," she says. The twenty-three-year-old is now a proud member of Albuquerque's Duke City Derby and skates on two teams: the Muñeca Muertas (the league's travel team) as well as the HoBots.

As her love of the game grew, so did her family's. "Everyone kinda raises their eyebrows and nods their heads incredulously until they see a game. Then they're hooked too!" she says. Her boyfriend even braved a family reunion solo because Dai Zovi was out of town attending a meeting of the Women's Flat Track Derby Association. "We were already in the process of starting the league by the time I met my boyfriend, so it wasn't a negotiable item," she says.

The fun inherent in the athleticism of derby isn't lost on Dai Zovi. She has several good friends on the league, one of whom is on an opposing team. "She hits so, so, so hard," Dai Zovi says of her friend-turned-nemesis on the track. "When I think about our last game against each other, I think the most fun I had was the times when I was mad at her, like when I sat in the penalty box for trying to fight her (she didn't fight back) and every time she skated by me she pointed and laughed."

You'll find teams celebrating after dominating an entire bout or even just a few jams. (left)

When Calvello died in May 2006, a skate-shaped cloud hung over rinks across the nation. Derby girls mourned the sport's loss and held fundraisers and screenings of the documentary based on her life, *Demon of the Derby*. Calvello used to say there was a little bit of her in all of the girls doing it today, and it seems the skaters agree.

But Ann Calvello isn't the only role model to rise up from the ashes of the sport's past and make an impact on the current revival. Lorretta "Little Iodine" Behrens is as boisterous an advocate of derby now as she was when she skated in the sixties. Behrens, who stands five feet tall, is a feisty, red-headed, outspoken living legend who can still get on her skates—and does—with the help of a walker.

"I'm here for this reason: to see the future grow. Today's skaters are living on a name that was made to last for all generations—roller derby skated by roller gals," says Behrens. A one-time formidable blocker, Behrens is still well known among fan groups and old-time skaters. She can frequently be seen at Sin City Rollergirls' practices and on the sideline during games in Vegas—hip-checking skaters before they hit the track, doling out advice on proper blocking techniques, and letting everyone know exactly what's on her mind.

"I have to say I was thrilled to have the flat-track league from Atlanta have a 'Little Iodine' championship game in my name," Behrens says. "I give thanks for the gals who keep in touch."

Ann Calvello and Lorretta Behrens may have been the bad girls of derby, but just as it is now as it was then, there were good girls among them, too. The Bay Bombers' Joanie Weston is still remembered as derby's "Golden Girl."

CAREFUL WHAT YOU SAY TO THE QUEEN

Maisha "Queen Loseyateefa" Smith didn't always dream of being a roller girl. In fact, after reading an article about her local league, the Atlanta Rollergirls, she showed up at practice with the hopes of being a water girl or a towel holder. "But I was told I could actually skate, and I've been going ever since," explains Smith.

At age thirty, Smith skates for the Altanta Rollergirls' Toxic Shocks team and says her reserved nature off the track works for her on the track, as people often mistake her quietness as meanness. That said, Smith appreciates the aggressive side of the sport. "I love that I can knock your ass over today and chill with you tomorrow," she says of her sisters in skates.

And there's only one thing Smith would change about the sport: "Losing. I love my league and want everyone to be successful, but I want to win more."

If the fans' collective love can be judged by volume of mail and gifts, then Weston was the all-around most valuable player of her game. The blonde bomber's pigtails made her famous, and her skating ability made her a crowd favorite. Unlike Calvello, Weston hated being booed by the crowd. They were the perfect rivals, not to mention proof positive that in derby, it takes all kinds

BIRDS OF A FEATHER

Outwardly outrageous or not, women of all backgrounds, social statuses, sexual orientations, and ages are not only tolerated but welcomed in derby. Slogans like "Were you the only girl in the mosh pit?" and "We're pleased to beat you!" grace promotional fliers designed to quickly give wannabes a taste of what they could possibly be signing up for as a new recruit. Leagues make it clear that while all types of women are welcome, a desire to skate hard and fast and get out some aggression is always needed.

Sociologists could have a heyday putting roller derby under a microscope. As a culture unto itself, so many different aspects of community and social dynamics play into making it a success. Bonds form on the track in unpredictable pairs. Skaters who would likely never know each other had it not been for derby unite on the track and can't imagine skating with anyone else. It must be that women inevitably form a unique bond when they can hit each other as hard as possible one moment and then raise a glass together afterward, toasting the fiercest, most numbing blows.

As Ann Calvello once told *Metro Newspapers* about Joanie Weston, long-term rival and friend, "I never did hang around with a lot of women…but Joanie, Joanie used to surf the Pacific with no wetsuit. She was a fantastic athlete." Roller derby offers

As roller girls are fond of saying, derby is cheaper (and more effective) than anger-management classes. (above)

this beautiful duality of love and respect, despite what happens come bout time.

THAT'S WHAT ROLLER GIRLS
ARE MADE OF

Potentials of all shapes and sizes show up for recruitment nights and tryouts, hoping to lend something unique to a sport already infused with extreme attitude and talent. Many of the skaters come from lifelong athletic backgrounds and have played competitive, full-contact sports before strapping on their quads. But another faction of skaters is just as prominent: they own more cat-eye glasses than spandex, and they remember what it was like to be picked last on the playground.

Wherever and whomever, derby offers a spot for most skaters willing to put in the work. But that's just it: derby demands commitment and effort. Endurance, speed, and agility are required for all positions during the game. And not every woman has it when she walks through the door of a practice space.

Leagues have training teams that include their most talented and dedicated skaters. Some employ coaches—sports fanatics looking for a new way to put their strategic minds to use or ex-speed skaters who adapt their training methods for derby. Most believe they can make a derby girl out of anyone with basic skating skills and the time and desire to make every practice and meeting.

Roller girl recruitment methods are developed, for the most part, around the laws of supply and demand. Leagues just starting up, with little presence in their marketplaces, are often more apt to extend few requirements for becoming part of a team.

They may impose little beyond an age limit and practice attendance requirements.

As league founders build their ranks, however, and team spots
are filled, tryouts often become necessary. Those looking to join
the rapidly growing, rowdy groups of femmes must be excep-
tional not only in their wheels but in their mindset—leagues
looking for a higher level of talent will run potential skaters
through a series of drills, including question-and-answer-type
sessions surrounding their views of the sport. Tryouts, however, don't mean a girl is automatically sized up, eliminated, or
accepted; each skater is evaluated on a variety of characteristics,
ability being first and foremost.

*Practice requires skating drills
both on and off of quads.
(above)*

on passing tryouts, skaters are put through the paces in a
training period that tests their will, strength, and dedication, after
which they may claim their derby name and be placed on a team.

"The number one determining factor of derby ability is dedication. Almost any girl who puts in the time and tries hard at
every practice develops into a strong player. It's awesome to see,"
says Ivana Clobber of the Boston Derby Dames.

Roller derby leagues operate on a strict do-it-yourself, grassroots
ethic with regards to league meetings, team meetings, and
get-togethers between the individual committees running each
organization. Leagues are incorporated within their respective
states and most are skater-owned and skater-run. That means

that the skaters themselves are in control of all business aspects, including paying taxes, filing for incorporation, instituting bylaws, negotiating contracts with rink owners, arranging for promotions and public relations opportunities, working with charities, and every other aspect that goes into running an organization. Not to mention organizing, staffing, running, and acting as the main attraction for the best bouts possible.

EQUAL PARTS FEISTY

AND FEARLESS

Not everyone understands the allure of roller derby. Put a group of roller girls within arm's reach and heads begin to nod, fists begin to pump, and a commonality is reinforced.

"I can't imagine, nor do I want to, *not* playing roller derby or being a roller girl," says Tia "TNTia" Cook of Arizona Roller Derby's Tent City Terrors. "Every woman has a little derby in 'em."

As we've pointed out, derby girls vary in background, but there are some commonalities, like the love of their wheels flying across the floor, their teammates within arm's reach, or bracing for a hit at any moment that could land them on the ground. Roller derby is a full-contact sport, and while skaters train hard, wear protective gear, and are bound by a strict set of governing rules, the hits are real. And roller girls love the adrenaline rush of giving them and taking them.

One thing all bouts have in common is fierce competition. And a win never comes easy. Roller girls' pride in their teams is as big as the trophies, shown here by the Gotham Girls. (below left)

As for appearance, ask the skaters who practice hours and hours each week to describe their uniforms and they can sum them up in a sentence or two. While sexy and cute, they aren't the reason for the girls' presence. Ask instead why she plays the game, why she loves it so, why it's unique, and you could be tied up in conversation for the rest of the evening.

"It's like being in rehab together," says Jen "She Who Cannot Be Named" Frale of Denver's Rocky Mountain Rollergirls. "Derby's like a drug. And you know it when you've met others who are addicted and can't quit. You travel all around the country, you meet all of these interesting women, and you think, 'Oh god. You're on it, too.'"

FIRST BLOOD

If she lacks confidence when she hits the track, a roller girl will adopt it soon enough. Leagues take care to ensure that newbies have the basics of the game down and enough skill to absorb full-force hits while on eight wheels, but all the watching in the world can't compare to what it's like taking a hit. And the first one always comes.

Absorbing that first blow, or at the very least recovering from it, changes a skater. It changes the way she carries herself, navigates the world outside the rink, and handles everyday obstacles. In short, it changes her view of herself. Most skaters can tell you about the story that led to their understanding of the art of the block. It's a great source of pride.

There are only so many hits skaters will withstand before they learn to retaliate. Prowess on the track is how skaters earn their stars and stripes—their reputations precede them within their own leagues, and word can and does spread nationwide about who is the most agile, who skates the fastest, and who delivers the deadliest blows. Derby girls form their opinions and size each other up long before taking to the track together.

So when it comes to the roller girl alter ego, the insecure routine gets left behind, a necessity when it comes to doing what they do in front of large crowds of fans. Derby girls must simultaneously crave the crowd and be able to ignore it. They must retreat inside their heads to a quietness that enables them to think strategically, both offensively and defensively, in the midst of rowdy fans screaming their names, surrounding the track, and downing cans of beer. Roller girls skate as much for themselves and the love of the game as they do for ticket sales. After all, there is no

Derby dames are always looking for an edge and, accordingly, her quads are an investment. Serious thought and time are put into the purchase and upkeep of trucks, boots, bearings, and wheels. (above)

Special training exercises are developed to teach skaters how to play in close quarters and to maintain a tight pack. (left)

guarantee of crowds. The skaters who started the roller derby revival had no idea how the public would react. Yet, they kept at it, because, whether fans responded or not, derby is a sport skaters simply fall in love with. In reality, the skaters are there for the same reasons as the fans are: action, aggression, and contact.

The women of derby aren't professional skaters. Roller girls live in your neighborhood, they shop at your grocery store, and they work in your office. They may even be teaching your kids.

Whatever the case, roller girls are well aware of their personas and make no excuses about their conduct, dress, or attitude. After all, derby has never been a quiet sport.

Jammers, indicated by the star on their helmet, score the points, thus leaving them the target for some of the most aggressive blocking. (below)

Roller girls fight fiercely on the track for a win. But after the bout, the sisterhood is only solidified by the competition. (right)

5

YEAH, BUT IS IT REAL?

The only thing that makes a roller girl's blood boil faster than an illegal block is the question "Is it really real?" A holdover belief from the old days, many a spectator still walk in to modern-day matches wondering if the scores and fights are predetermined.

While it may be hard to believe such rough-and-tumble action is real, spend a week with any league in the country and you'll find out it is indeed. Sure, an element of theatrics is part of the game—from the uniforms to the skaters' alter egos, there's no denying it. But audience members who only see bouts (and not all the practice time leading up to them) may not realize that the performance aspect of the game always takes a backseat to the skating.

"Part of the performance is in the physical competition of the sport…. This allows the ordinary little middle-school teacher by day to become a rowdy roller derby queen on wheels by night," says Janet "Hellen Wheels" Clarke of Arizona Roller Derby.

Athleticism and brawn form the less publicized side of a sport known for trash talking, knock downs, and careening legs in fishnets. Being a performer is not what derby girls spend hours each week practicing—that's just a side of themselves they show once a month (if that) at a bout. The rest of their efforts are spent strategizing, executing, and raising their abilities to new levels. Every skater steps on the track during a bout knowing that if they want their team to win, they'll have to earn it.

"How you can dismiss a sport that has unified nearly 2,000 women across the country into a common unit?" asks Jennifer "Kasey Bomber" Barbee of the LA Derby Dolls. "We all take the strength this sport has given us into other parts of our lives to get what we really, really want because dammit, derby taught us that we deserve it."

Skaters will, literally, put themselves in harm's way to keep the opposing team's jammer from getting by and scoring a point. (below)

The rock star, alter-ego element of derby allows for women to find their inner release…sometimes releasing it on an opponent. (right)

With feelings that intense infused into the sport, it's no wonder that this level of passion manifests itself on the rink not only in the form of hip checks and shoulder throws but also in fights.

"I've had a broken lip, kicked shins, elbows in the face, and kicks to the groin," says coach Pauly Perez, head referee for the Arizona Roller Derby, "all because a skater felt that strongly about a call I made. The bottom line, however, is this: there's a time to fight for how you feel and a time to play by the rules as defined by your league. As skaters go through their careers, they learn the difference."

THE LAW

Roller derby referees have nearly as big a commitment to the game as the skaters. They are required to understand every nuance of the sport and be able to explain it to a very angry penalized skater in the middle of a frenzied crowd.

To minimize the impact on referees and ensure they can focus solely on the game, only team captains are permitted to talk to the referees during a bout. Captains are responsible for disputing any penalties, calling timeouts, and fraternizing with the law, who keep points, track penalties, and dole out any necessary punishments. Nevertheless, it's hard to keep down a roller girl who believes she's been unfairly fouled and referees are repeatedly on the receiving end of their wrath.

At bouts, the skaters who've wracked up the most penalties on each team square off in a penalty game, this time it's a game of arm wrestling. (above)

As with any sport, refs have the hardest job. Ultimately they're the ones responsible for a clean, fair bout. (below)

So how do refs learn the rules of the road, keep their cool, and keep hell on wheels in check? It helps that many referees are ex-derby girls—skaters who have been forced to move on due to life circumstances or injury. Oftentimes, skaters who can no longer make the magnificent commitment required to be a roller girl, but don't want to step away from the sport completely, transition into the shot-calling role.

"When I retired from skating, the girls asked if I could instead assume the role of head referee, and I accepted. It has been quite the learning process, but I would do anything for those girls," says Heather "Betsy Blackheart" Dalton of Denver's Rocky Mountain Rollergirls.

Men who catch the derby bug are also drawn to the role of referee. Male referees come from all walks of life—ex-speed skaters, hockey players, and the occasional significant other of a

LAW SCHOOL OR ROLLER DERBY?

How could a derby girl choose between the two? If you ask Julia "Red Dragon" Vendeland, a forty-two-year-old skater for the Pikes Peak Derby Dames, well, pretty easily. Derby is the easy winner.

Vendeland heard a few of the Pikes Peak Derby Dames doing a radio interview, showed up for a practice, and was hooked. "I had recently and finally made the decision to go back to college to finish my degree with an eye toward law school and knew that there was no way I could fully commit to the time requirements to be successful at both activities," says Vendeland. "At that time, I was forty-one and knew realistically that I only had a few years left to play a full-contact combat sport. So I chose roller derby."

Vendeland's hubbie, who has earned the derby name "Dragon Tamer," was supportive and has gone along for the ride. "He knows he married an athlete and is understanding of all of the time and commitment that it requires," explains Vendeland. "He's tolerant of my stinky socks and sweaty clothes, but thinks it's gross when I wash my pads in the dishwasher (they come out so lemony fresh that way)."

And there's no looking back for Vendeland or her family. She's gained far too much. Ask her what she loves about derby and the answer comes easily: "Everything," she says.

roller girl. Some leagues have rules against fraternizing with the referees, but plenty allow significant others of derby dames into the family fold. In addition, many are ex-jocks and can lend their strategizing and team-building skills to leagues.

Regardless of how they get involved, there's no downplaying the referees' commitment or place within their leagues, and they're doing it without the limelight and glory that the derby girls receive. Even in the shadows, referees are developing a culture of their own, one based on rules and the betterment of the sport. They lend a unique perspective to the girls behind the driving force of the revival. They too sacrifice time away from work, families, and their own hobbies to debate the pros and cons of certain rulings, create the most efficient methods of tracking penalties and points, and standardize the way they do things in preparation for a true nationwide interleague resurgence.

FIGHT CLUB

With all this intense devotion to derby, it's no wonder that what may appear to an outsider as merely a hobby can actually come to fisticuffs on the track. It's not unusual for jams to be interrupted by two skaters from opposing teams duking it out right there in the thick of it. Sometimes, in extreme cases where one skater is outnumbered by members of an opposing team, dogpiles will completely disrupt a jam, with all of the skaters forgoing points scoring for bloodlust.

Roller girls train to stay on their feet, take other skaters down safely in the event of a brawl, and get hit repeatedly while keeping their tempers in check. But when the whistle signals the start of a jam, all bets are off.

The rules governing what skaters *can't* do are perhaps even more clear than those dictating what they can do. An errant forearm or closed fist can cause enough rancor for all skaters involved to end up on the floor.

So, yes, fighting happens in roller derby just the way it does in other highly physical sports. Do refs encourage it? Absolutely not. Do fans egg on the players? Hell yes. Recovering from fights and going back to their jobs as business partners is critical, however, for roller girls. Leagues work to create a culture where skaters can work together and be respectful of the sport and each other, which is why roller girls have adopted the standing motto of "What happens on the track, stays on the track!"

In the past, fights could also be used strategically. There's no other surefire way to close the gap during a tight bout than to sacrifice time in the penalty box in exchange for taking down an opposing team's jammer with a fight. It prevents her from scoring any more points for the duration of the jam.

The Lonestar Rollergirls discourage the use of fighting as strategy and have methods that ultimately penalize the fighters. For instance, if a fight breaks out during a jam and the jammer

A jammer surrounded by the opposing team's players is an unhappy jammer. She's got a tough job ahead of her—pass all of them to score points for her team. (above)

is not involved, the jam continues. Any team whose players are involved in the fighting are forced to play short as long as it continues. The Lonestar Rollergirls have an unspoken sisterly understanding that while battles do occur, no one should be seriously trying to hurt each other.

Nonetheless, skater Amanda "Sissy Spankit" Deal, a twenty-five-year-old who holds three jobs in addition to skating, offers, "It's roller derby, that's how it's supposed to be played…fun and dirty. If it wasn't for the dirty players or mischievous players it wouldn't be as exciting or fun for us or the crowd. If it wasn't for the fighting and flare of the girls, I don't think I would have ever joined."

Some players think it undermines the game, though. "We hardly fight now that our game has improved. And we would never fight in a close game; we wouldn't want to skate short," says Denise "Ivanna S. Pankin" Grimes of the Sin City Rollergirls.

"People talk about the legitimacy of roller derby, and fighting takes away from that. The skill level of the skaters should be enough to keep the crowd completely enraptured," says Dale "Black Dahlia" Rio. "With the Derby Dolls, the lack of fights certainly isn't an issue. At our banked-track bouts, the audience walks away absolutely mind-blown and impressed by the athleticism and skill of the skaters."

For some leagues, penalties for fighting are becoming more and more stringent. These days, they can far outweigh any potential benefits gained by strategically thrown punches. In fact, skaters can be completely booted from games for fighting or other unsportswomanlike behavior.

FROM BOARDING
TO ROLLING

Twenty-five-year-old Carolyn "C-Roll" Kunkel is into anything fast. Professional mountain boarder, amateur snowboarder, and roller girl, C-Roll does it all. "Roller derby seems to be taking over my life. I love this sport. It's awesome to be playing and skating hard and hanging out with a bunch of cool chicks who are tough and dedicated to the sport," she offers. Besides, C-Roll credits the Long Island Roller Rebels' aggressive training schedule with keeping her in the tip-top shape she needs to be in to participate in all of the other sports she loves.

As for everyone else involved in C-Roll's active life, they're as supportive of her derby career as they have been of her other activities. "The people around me think it's pretty sweet that I'm a roller girl and usually come down and watch the bouts," she says. "Sometimes when people hear that I skate they ask how I can be so small and still play such an aggressive sport," C-Roll laughs. "I tell them to come to a bout and see—I'm the one who scores the points!"

"I think that the more athletically skilled a team or league gets, the fewer big fights we will see break out," says Nikkie "Anita Drink" Busch, a referee for the Mad Rollin' Dolls of Madison, Wisconsin. "Players still regularly try to get away with what they can and risk fouls when it's to their strategic advantage to do so. It's certainly not a boring sport to watch, that's for sure!"

TOUGH LOVE

In roller derby, skaters don't ask if they'll get hurt; they simply await the pain. It's a tough sport, and pulled muscles, strains, sprains, bruises, the occasional shiner, and even broken bones are part of the risk.

Falls come with a bruise or scrape, which derby girls wear with pride, showing them off at afterparties, during prepractice stretching, and anywhere else the urge to make a fall worth its salt known. One girl even adopted her derby moniker courtesy of an injury: Natily "Ginger Snap" Blair of the Gotham Girls Roller Derby in New York is a fiery redhead who earned her name when she broke her arm with a resounding "snap."

It's no wonder protective gear is required from top to bottom—wrist, knee, and elbow pads in addition to mouth guards and helmets. However, there is no protective gear designed specifically for derby's impacts. Most roller girls choose skateboarding equipment, replacing cracked guards and wear and tear more often than skateboarders!

But there are also endless drills for how to fall just so. Derby dames actually fall on purpose over and over in an effort to strengthen their muscle memory and limit the likelihood of injuries, or at least lessen their severity.

"The first time I ever scrimmaged in a practice, I got a head of steam up as the jammer and knocked down three to four girls like a bowling ball!" says Janet "Hellen Wheels" Clarke of Arizona Roller Derby. "Once the girls realized that I could hold my own on skates, they dished it right back. I remember getting a floor burn on the front of my left leg that lasted for weeks."

Rink rash and fishnet burn are common (and relatively easy to heal). They're the byproduct of exposed flesh meeting the rink in a way that creates a grate-type pattern in the flesh that hurts much more than appearances may lead derby laymen to believe. The TXRD Lonestar Rollergirls make the following distinctions:

Shots to the face are illegal in the vast majority of roller derby leagues, but within the mayhem of a pack, they can and do occur. (right)

Track Rash or Masonite Burn: Stinging, red streak across buttocks and/or legs resulting from too-short-skirts/pants/shorts and exposed skin hitting the banked track. Accompanied by painful skin-sticking-to-masonite board sound.

Fishnet Burn: Similar to Masonite Burn, but an attractive, semipermanent fish-scale pattern resulting from falling while wearing fishnet stockings.

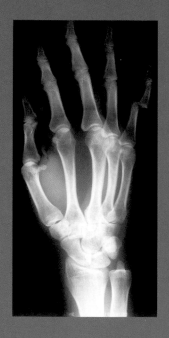

More serious injuries can also occur in derby—costly, painful ones that can keep skaters out of the game for months and sometimes end their career. Using the Minnesota RollerGirls as an example, some of their more serious battle scars (both from practices and bouts) include torn miniscus; torn PCLs, MCLs, and ACLs (who ever knew there were "CLs" other than the "ACL"); broken ankles, tailbones, and collar bones; two spiral fractures on one leg; numerous dislocated shoulders; and all kinds of fishnet-shaped floor burns.

Then there are the fearless skaters of the banked track, who don't get off much easier. Repetitive falling drills coupled with actual falls during bouts and practices put considerable strain on skaters' knees. Punky Bruiser and Ms. Conduct, both Lonestar Rollergirls, had a stint watching bouts from the sidelines, knees wrapped up and skates off. Bruiser says she didn't at first realize the severity of her injury, but eventually succumbed to surgery when she learned of her torn meniscus and loosened cartilage. Still, on May 7, 2006, six months after she sustained the injury, Bruiser fans reveled in the skater's return as she bouted with her team, the Holy Rollers, against TXRD's Hell Cats.

SPOTLIGHT ON LUCY BALL-BREAKER

By night, thirty-three-year-old Mary Kruger morphs into LA Derby Dolls' skater Lucy Ball-Breaker as she laces up her skates and hops on to the banked track. Kruger didn't fully understand what the revival of the sport meant when she signed on, but nonetheless, she showed up to practice. "It didn't take long before we were a group of forty to fifty women learning how to skate and tap in to our aggression. I found myself in the middle of all these strong, interesting, amazing women who I knew would become my friends, and I was hooked!"

Today, Kruger is a force to be reckoned with on the track. She's known as the "Dominatrix of the Derby" and the "Temptress of Torture." According to her team, Kruger has three favorite sounds: the roar of the crowd, the crack of the whip, and the whimper of a groveling rival.

Initially, her mom worried about the likelihood of injury. But Kruger persisted. "I say it's worth it! Bring it on, I can take it!" After all, in Kruger's eyes, she has much more to gain than lose from the sport she loves so dearly. "It allows women to be everything their mother raised them not to be: fast, rough, arrogant, naughty, mean, and ballsy," she says. "And the women I've met in this sport are becoming the most amazing friends I've ever had."

But joint damage isn't the only injury featured in league "scrape-books." Perhaps one of the most famous injuries to date, at least among her peers, happened to Sara Jean "Mad Maxine" Jeromin of the Bay Area Derby Girls. During an endurance drill, Maxine slid face-first into the hard acrylic rink enclosures surrounding the rink where her league practices. The paralegal by day cracked both front teeth and had the presence of mind, at least according to derby lore (and one newspaper article), to collect herself and snap a shot of the damage with her camera phone.

Eventually, Maxine's two front teeth were extracted, and roller girl message boards and online blogs exploded with not only photos of the damage but also pleas for donations to help Maxine buy new teeth. Roller girls across the nation rallied together to help Maxine out.

And that's just practice! The most serious injuries occur at bouts, when tempers really flair and competition is at an all-time high. Leagues make certain to have trained and certified medical staff on hand to deal with minor injuries and keep skaters calm in the event of more serious mishaps. In fact, certain leagues have even taken to allowing EMTs into bouts for free.

The second period of an Atlanta Rollergirls' bout called for serious medical attention when Destructiva, star jammer of the Sake Tuyas, landed in a pileup of skaters and suffered two broken ribs. The bout took its toll on both teams, however, with two members of the Apocolypstix (Peach Clobber and Susan B. Agony) taken out of the game when they sustained serious back injuries. But the most memorable damage of the night quite possibly went to Big Red of the Sake Tuyas, who broke her index finger, taped it up, wrote "Destructiva" on it, and kept skating.

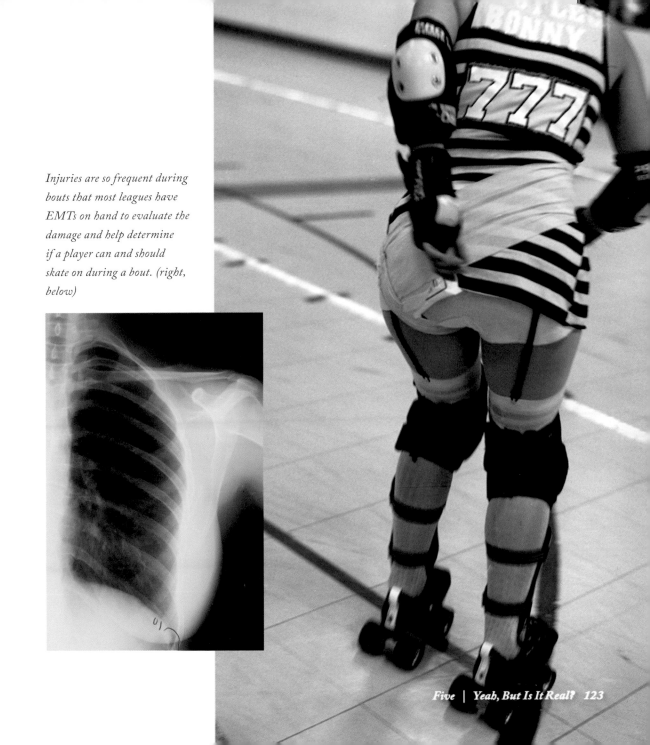

Injuries are so frequent during bouts that most leagues have EMTs on hand to evaluate the damage and help determine if a player can and should skate on during a bout. (right, below)

Roller girls are proud of the bumps and lumps they earn. They're a badge of honor, literally, for some leagues such as the TXRD Lonestar Rollergirls, who crown the skater with the most substantial injury of the year with the Purple Heart award. The award most often goes to a skater with a broken bone.

Derby begins where insurance lets off. Early on in the rebirth of the sport, the need for secondary insurance became clear when an uninsured Texas skater suffered a very serious injury. Many leagues today require primary insurance as well as a special form of insurance that covers skaters for derby-related injuries that go beyond, in terms of cost, what their primary insurance is willing to handle.

What sets derby girls apart from the masses? They get the hell beaten out of them for no pay, little bits of glory, sacrificed personal time…all for the love of derby.

Roller girls wear their injuries like a badge of pride. Some leagues even present a skater with the worst injury of a season with a Purple Heart Award. (above)

Referees are as much a part of any roller derby league as the skaters. As such, they are the family members roller girls love to hate! (left)

The jam goes on, even when a pileup temporarily stops its momentum. (right)

6

CAN THEY DO THAT?

Why is that team skating with one less girl? Was that clothesline legal? Why's that skater in the penalty box? What's with the jammer putting her hands on her hips all the time? Why do jammers have stars on their helmets?

Roller derby may, to the untrained eye, look like choreographed mayhem, but it's far from it. It's actually a very structured sport with intricate rules and strict etiquette. Here's a primer on some of the good stuff.

ROLLER DERBY IN A NUTSHELL

Leagues vary the rules that they use, but the general guidelines and overall object of the game—flat and banked—remain the same: roller derby is still, in essence, a race.

Pivots set the pace and act as the last line of defense. Blockers try to get their team's jammer through the pack while preventing the other team's jammer from getting through. Jammers are responsible for scoring points. The jammers must get through the pack in bounds to score. They score points for each member of the opposing team whom they pass in bounds.

THE TRACK

Flat tracks are marked directly on the ground with rope, rope lights, tape, or cones so the crowd (and the refs) knows whether skaters are in bounds, an important facet of the game when it comes to scorekeeping and legal versus illegal blocking. Fans are generally invited to begin seating approximately ten feet away from the track. Many leagues make note of high-traffic areas in the seating area where skaters seem to fly from the track easily—also known as "bodybag boulevard." Chairs are sometimes present, but for the best seats in the house, sit directly on the floor.

Since the banked track is elevated, it is generally surrounded by bleachers. This vantage gives onlookers a good view of the action as well as front-row seating when the skaters enter the track or get thrown over the railing. Skaters train to skate high on the straighter portion of the track and get closer to the inside around turns. This enables them to get the most momentum, propel themselves farther, and remain on the track.

THE POSITIONS

At the start of a jam, **pivots** are the skaters at the front of the pack wearing helmet covers with a stripe down the middle. Pivots keep the pace of the pack, slowing and speeding things up to enable their jammer to score the maximum number of points. They also act as the last line of defense.

Three **blockers** from each team make up the bulk of the pack. Their job is to fuse offense and defense simultaneously. Blockers work hard to get their jammer through the pack, past the other team's blockers, while at the same time preventing the opposing team's jammer from getting through. These are the heavy hitters.

A maximum of one **jammer** from each team is allowed on the track during play. Jammers, who wear stars on their helmets, line up at the rear of the pack. Jammers start at the second whistle and work to make their way through the pack, lap it, and do it again (as many times as they can). They score points on the opposing team members they pass while skating in bounds.

Jammers do not score their first time through the pack. On their second pass, jammers score points by legally passing opponents while in bounds.

FLAT-TRACK SCORING, BLOCKING, AND PENALTIES

The Women's Flat Track Derby Association (WFTDA) has established a set of standardized flat-track rules, although many leagues finesse the rules to work with their organization's preferences. WFTDA works continually on and releases periodically a set of rules that are widely used by flat-track leagues across the country during both interleague and home-team play.

The following highlights the key WFTDA rules, but bout-goers are urged to pay attention to the variations played out before them. Like roller girls, no two bouts are necessarily the same.

The skaters of the Arizona Roller Derby play by the rules of the Women's Flat Track Derby Association. (left)

BOUT STRUCTURE

Games are composed of three periods lasting twenty minutes each. WFTDA rules dictate that an unlimited number of jams can occur per period.

Jams last a maximum of two minutes. In between jams, skaters have twenty to thirty seconds to get in formation. If skaters are not in formation in the time allotted, teams may have to skate short or assume penalties. During the bout, there are no rules governing control of the inside of the track by specific positions.

SCORING

The basics of scoring:

- After clearing the pack the first time, jammers score points by legally passing opponents in bounds. A "pass" is determined by a skater's hips.

- Designated jammers are the only scoring players on the track in each jam.

- Pivots may become jammers during the course of a jam, replacing their team's jammer as the scoring player (see Passing the Star).

- In order to accrue points for passed skaters, a jammer must pass opposing skaters legally, without committing penalties against them.

- Jammers may score on opponents in the penalty box having passed in bounds and scored upon all other opposing blockers on the track.

- Jammers score points upon passing all opponents, including those who have been knocked to the floor or are out of bounds.

Lead Jammer: The first jammer to make it through the pack while remaining in bounds and without committing penalties against the skaters she's passing is designated as the lead jammer (the second jammer through the pack can assume lead jammer status if she meets these requirements during the jam when the first jammer through the pack does not). If neither jammer meets the criteria, there will be no lead jammer designated for the jam. The lead jammer can call off a jam by placing her hands on her hips before the two-minute time period is up to prevent the other team's jammer from accumulating points. Referees indicate lead jammer status by forming an "L" with their hand.

Passing the Star: As long as she's already made it through the pack once, the jammer can remove her helmet cover and pass it to her team's pivot, who will then become the point scorer. This is a risky but strategic move used when the jammer is tangled up in the pack or when the jammer needs a break.

Grand Slam: If one jammer completely laps the opposing jammer, she will score one additional point. When the opposing jammer is in the penalty box, the additional point is awarded each time the scoring jammer breaks through the pack.

BLOCKING

Blocking is any movement on the track designed to impede or dislocate an opponent. A skater can block an opposing player at any time during game play, and can knock an opposing skater down or out of bounds, or impede her speed or movement through the pack.

A pivot and a blocker team up to simultaneously protect their jammer and assist her in getting through the pack. (above)

Here are a few of the restrictions the WFTDA imposes on blocking:

- Legal blocks can not fall above the shoulders, below the hips, or on the back of the skater being blocked.

- Skaters can block using shoulders and arms above the elbow.

- Legs may not be used to intentionally make contact in blocking.

- When engaging another skater, skaters can not swing their elbows with a forward or backward motion or cock them for extra force.

- When engaging another skater, elbows also can not be swung with upward or downward motion.

- Elbows must be bent when blocking; using arms and jabbing is not allowed.

- Hooking (drawing the arm through the opponent's arm) is not permitted.

- Skaters can not use their forearms to push. Forearms can only be used to absorb the force of a lateral block initiated by another skater.

Even then, the skater's arms must be pulled in toward the body.

- A skater's forearms may never legally contact an opposing skater's back.

- Skaters must be in bounds when executing a block. They must also be in bounds when initiating a block and are not permitted to pick up momentum from outside of bounds in order to execute a block.

- Blocking a skater who is out of bounds is not permitted.

- Skaters must have at least one skate on the floor when executing a block.

- Skaters can not be down or at a standstill when executing a block, nor can they execute a block on an opponent who is down.

- Use of hands is not permitted.

- Tripping or falling intentionally in front of another skater will result in a penalty.

- Skaters may not join arms or hands in a multiple-player block.

PENALTIES

Skaters and teams are assessed penalties due to infractions that are illegal. Referees signal penalties as they occur during the jam. No team may have more than two skaters sitting out at a time. If a team has more than two skaters being assessed penalties that result in skaters sitting out of a jam, the penalties will be served consecutively (i.e., the third skater will sit out once the first skater has served her penalty). A team that has a skater expelled from the period or game finishes the jam and plays the next jam short that player, then may put in another skater to replace her from the next jam on.

Penalties are cumulative for the entire bout (i.e., minor penalties are not "reset" between periods or before overtime). Penalties do not carry over from bout to bout.

Here is a sampling of penalties as dictated by the WFTDA:

- False start

- Too many skaters on the rink

- Improper uniform, jewelry, or skates

- Failure to use helmet covers

- Gross unsportsladylike conduct

- Illegal interference in game play by skaters not involved in the jam

- Insubordination to a referee

- Fighting

- Any form of illegal blocking that is deemed a serious threat to other skaters, such as blocks falling above the shoulders or below the hips

- Any form of illegal blocking that is not deemed a serious threat to other skaters

- Blocking or assisting outside the pack

- Intentionally cutting the track

- Intentionally skating out of bounds

- Hitting or punching to the face

- Kicking another skater

- Intentional tripping with feet or hands

- Choking by helmet straps

- Biting

- Intentional, negligent, or reckless blocking to the head or neck

- Intentional, negligent, or reckless pulling of the head, neck, or helmet

- Jumping onto or into a pile of fighting skaters ("dogpile")

- Serious physical violence or any action deemed by the officials to cause an extraordinary physical threat

- Teams may be assessed penalties for illegal procedure

OVERTIME

If the score is tied at the end of a bout, a final overtime jam will determine the winner. After one minute to regroup, the teams skate a full two-minute jam. This jam has no lead jammer, and penalties may be called during it. The team with the most points at the end of the overtime jam is the bout winner. If the score is still tied, additional jams are played until the tie is broken.

BANKED-TRACK SCORING, BLOCKING, AND PENALTIES

Banked-track leagues develop their own league-specific doctrine, so it is impossible to list one solitary, concise set of banked rules. However, the LA Derby Dolls agreed to share their take on the game as an example of what to possibly expect at a banked-track bout.

BOUT STRUCTURE

Games are composed of two periods. A period is twenty minutes of running time. The period clock may only be stopped for official time-outs. An unlimited number of jams are allowed within each period. A jam can last up to one minute. Between jams, a team has thirty seconds to get into formation.

Jammer Positioning: At the start of the game, the high- or low-track jammer starting position will be determined by a coin toss. Throughout the game, the team that scores the most points in the previous jam will have first choice of whether their jammer will start on the high or low side of the track.

SCORING

The basics of scoring:

- After clearing the pack the first time, jammers score points by passing opponents with no part of their skates touching the ground outside the boundaries of the track. A pass is determined by a skater's hips. She scores points against the opposing team's skaters each time she laps them after the first pass.

- Jammers may score one point on an opponent in the penalty box when the opposing team is short a blocker, after having lapped all of the opposing team, including the jammer, if there is one.

- Jammers may score on all opponents, including those who have been knocked to the floor or out of bounds.

- Jammers earn one point for each time they lap an opposing jammer.

- Penalties only affect the resulting score of a jam when a major penalty results in preventing a jammer from scoring.

- If a major penalty prevents a jammer from scoring, her team is awarded the full number of points she would have been eligible to receive had she been able to complete the jam. If the opposing team has a player in the penalty box, she is awarded the "ghost point" for that player, and if the opposing team's jammer fails to exit the pack on the first pass through the pack, the skater who has been fouled and her team are awarded that point as well (for a maximum of four points).

- If the jammer is scoring in the pack and a blocker goes beyond twenty feet in front of the pack when the jammer is in a position to score against her, the blocker receives a major penalty and the jammer's team receives a point for that blocker.

◯ If a blocker leaves the pack to follow the jammer around the pack while the jammer is making a scoring lap, the jammer scores on that blocker the moment the jammer is within twenty feet of the back of the pack. The blocker receives a major penalty.

◯ If the blocker ceases forward movement and rejoins the pack by allowing the pack to catch up with her while the jammer is scoring, the jammer's team may not receive an additional point for passing that blocker once a "blocker out of position" point has been awarded. The jammer's team may not score an additional point on that same blocker if the blocker skates forward and joins the back of the pack.

Lead Jammer: Lead jammer is a strategic position that is awarded to the jammer who is in the lead, having passed all of the blockers in the pack once. At all times during the jam, this lead may be challenged and obtained when the lead jammer is passed by the jammer from the opposing team. The

lead jammer is the only player who may end the jam at any time by placing both of her hands on her hips. The jam is only ended, however, when the referee blows the signal to end the jam.

A lead jammer may not call off the jam if she has fallen and any other part of her body besides her feet is touching the track surface, or if she is outside of the track's boundaries.

BLOCKING

Blocking is any movement on the track intended to impede or dislocate an opponent. Blockers may begin blocking opponents at any time after the jammer starting signal, except when they are outside the pack. Jammers may begin blocking any time after the jammer starting signal. Blocking is generally defined as contact between two players, but it can also include passive obstruction if a player is not within twenty feet of the pack.

Here are legal and illegal blocking maneuvers as defined by the LA Derby Dolls:

◯ Legal blocking zones apply to the body parts of the skater(s) initiating a block. Blocks may not fall above the shoulders, below the hips, or on the back of a skater.

- Blocking contact is allowed between the outer thighs of two skaters above the knee. Blocking is not permitted between the legs.

- Skaters may block using shoulders and arms above the elbow.

- Legs may not be used to make contact in blocking below the knee.

- Elbows may not contact another player. Contact may only begin in the area above the elbow, and contact must be maintained at all times between first upper arm contact and the elbow contact on the same arm. Skaters can not push opponents away with the elbow. The arm can not be extended from the body to block. No clotheslines are permitted. The point of the elbow can never make first contact with an opposing player (this includes any type of jabbing motion under any circumstances).

- Forearms may not be used in any first contact with an opposing player. Forearms may only contact another player if the first contact was with the arm between the elbow and shoulder, and the contact was maintained continuously. No part of the arm can be "hooked" underneath the arm of an opponent at any time. "Hooking" is defined as a blocker's arm falling between the opponent's arm in the area between the elbow and shoulder and her body.

- Skaters may not use their head when blocking.

- Blocking from behind is not permitted.

- At no time may any part of a player's body contact an opponent's back.

- Skaters must be in bounds when executing a block.

- Skaters must be in bounds when initiating a block; skaters may not pick up momentum for a block until in bounds. In bounds is defined as having both skates on the track.

- Skaters can't execute a block on a skater who is out of bounds.

- Skaters may not contact a player returning to the track until they are fully within the track's boundaries. If one skate is still on the infield, they are not fully within the track's boundaries.

- Skaters may not skate in a clockwise path on the track when blocking.

- Skaters may not touch, hold, or grab an opposing player with their hands or forearms.

- Skaters may perform "flying blocks," in which no part of their body or their skates are touching the track, so long as the contact with the other skater is otherwise legal.

- Skaters are permitted to block when they are at a full stop, as long as they are still within the pack.

- Skaters may not block when any part of their body besides their feet is contacting the track. This includes skaters who have fallen or are recovering from a fall.

- Skaters may not execute a block on a player who has any body part contacting the track. This includes skaters who have fallen, are recovering from a fall, or are in the process of falling.

- Skaters may not trip or intentionally fall in front of another skater.

- Skaters may not grasp arms, hands, or hold on to any body part (including hair) or item worn by a teammate (including safety equipment such as elbow or knee pads or wrist guards) in a multiple-player block that impedes a jammer at the connection point of the arms.

- Skaters from the same team are permitted to use their hands and forearms to shove their teammates into a jammer, so long as the contact with the jammer is otherwise legal.

PENALTIES

Penalties are tools of discipline for skaters and teams. Skaters and teams are assessed penalties due to infractions that are considered illegal.

The following infractions are considered illegal during a LA Derby Dolls' bout:

- False start

- Too many skaters on the track

- Improper uniform, jewelry, or skates

- Failure to properly secure safety equipment

- Gross unsportsladylike conduct

- Interference in game play by skaters not involved in the jam

- Deliberate and excessive insubordination to a referee

- Any form of illegal blocking that is deemed a serious threat to other skaters, such as blocks falling above the shoulders, between the legs, or below the knees

Padded bats deal out a banked-track penalty. (above)

- Any form of illegal blocking that results in the jammer falling

- Intentionally holding a jammer to the rail

- Intentionally preventing a jammer from getting up after a fall

- Intentional, negligent, or reckless blocking to the head or neck

- Intentional, negligent, or reckless pulling of the head, neck, or helmet

- Blocking after the jam has ended

- Any form of illegal blocking that does not significantly impact the outcome of the jam

- Blocking outside the pack

- Advancing on the infield or outfield (applies both to blockers and jammers)

- Minor use of forearms or hands (in which the opposing team's player does not fall)

- Intentionally skating out of bounds

Off the track, derby dames are the best of friends. On the track, well that's another story. (above)

FIGHTING

Any fighting, whether simulated or real, will result in immediate expulsion from the game. Further penalties may be assessed by the league, the gaming board, or the gaming commission against skaters and/or teams, and punishment may continue into future games or be defined by a period of time (weeks or months).

The team whose skaters are involved in a fight are assessed a major penalty. If assessing such a penalty on both teams results in both teams skating without a jammer, the teams serve the penalty in consecutive jams (one team without a jammer the next jam, the other without the jammer the following jam).

Ejected skaters may not return to the track for any reason, including team skate outs, and must remain in the dressing room for the remainder of the game.

In the moments before the whistle blows to signal the beginning of a jam, skaters must be on the track, in formation, and ready to roll. (left)

Only in derby can a pillow fight determine penalties. (right)

DERBY SLANG, AS DEFINED BY THE TXRD LONESTAR ROLLERGIRLS

Blood and Thunder or Queen of the Rink: Practice drill in which all skaters take the track and proceed to knock the hell out of each other until only one skater remains standing.

Cannonball: Deliberate fall to trip several skaters on the opposing team at once.

Clawing or Swimming: A jammer pulling her way through a tough pack.

Clothesline: Straight-arm block against a jammer's throat.

Cutting the track: Crossing the infield to rejoin the pack after you fall.

Fishnet burn: Similar to track rash, but an attractive, semipermanent fish-scale pattern resulting from falling while wearing fishnet stockings.

Give a whip: An assist move in which a skater extends her arm and whips her jammer around the track, propelling her with momentum and quite possibly taking out unsuspecting blockers in her path.

Over the top: Overhand cheat move in arm wrestling.

Snake drill: A practice drill in which all skaters skate single-file around the track while a single jammer weaves through the entire line from back to front.

Solid: A great compliment about a skater's stability and toughness.

Spank Alley: Where you go when you've been bad. Oftentimes, a penalty game during which a ref drags the most illegal skater down Spank Alley to be spanked by fans as she goes by.

Stich 'n Bitch: Team meeting where members get together to drink beer, work on uniforms, strategize, and basically, well, bitch.

- **T-stop:** Dragging the back skate perpendicular to the front skate.

- **Takedowns:** A safer version of "take that bitch down."

- **Take that bitch down:** A call to jump the jammer and stop her any way possible.

- **Thunderdome:** Where people go for roller derby mayhem and madness.

- **Track rash:** Stinging, red streak across buttocks and/or legs resulting from too-short-skirts/pants/shorts and exposed skin when falling.

- **Two-lap duel or match race:** Two skaters, two laps, anything goes.

OVERTIME

If the score is tied at the end of a bout, a final overtime jam determines the winner. After one minute to regroup, the teams skate a jam. Penalties may be called during the jam. If the score is still tied, additional jams are played until the tie is broken. The team with the most points at the end of the overtime jam(s) is declared the winner.

ROLL ON...

In roller derby, there are many nuances that affect point scoring, team formation, and the ultimate outcome. These intricacies are what really make the game interesting. From league to league, you'll see things done differently, so get out there, find the skaters tearing it up in your hometown, and learn how they play the game.

REFERENCES

ORGANIZATIONS

Blood and Thunder Magazine

www.bloodandthundermag.com

An organization that celebrates the accomplishments and memory of derby greats.

National Roller Derby Hall of Fame

www.rollerderbyhalloffame.com

An organization that celebrates the accomplishments and memory of derby greats.

National Museum of Roller Skating

www.rollerskatingmuseum.com

Located in Lincoln, Nebraska, this museum captures the history and future of roller skating.

RollerCon

www.rollercon.com

An annual roller derby convention.

Leadjammer

www.leadjammer.com

The most comprehensive source for derby news.

Roller Derby Preservation Association

www.rollerderbypreservationassociation.com

A group offering detailed information and press clippings on historical roller derby leagues.

RoxyRockett.com

A site dedicated to keeping roller derby a sport and not a spectacle.

Sin City Skates

www.sincityskates.com

A skater-run skate and equipment store.

International Rollergirls' Master Roster

www.twoevils.org/rollergirls

The official list of roller girl names.

Women's Flat Track Derby Association

www.wftda.com

The "by the skaters, for the skaters" governing body serving the flat-track roller derby community.

FILM

Demon of the Derby: The Ann Calvello Story

A cult favorite celebrating the one and only Ann Calvello.

The Fireball

Mickey Rooney stars as a boy who runs away to join the derby.

Hell on Wheels: The True Tale of All-Girl Roller Derby, Texas Style

A documentary detailing the resurrection of roller derby in Texas.

Jam

A professional film about the lives of derby skaters and promoters.

Kansas City Bomber

Raquel Welch stars as a derby dame trying to balance happiness with stardom.

Rollergirls

A&E produced thirteen one-hour, reality based episodes on the world of Texas derby.

Unholy Rollers: The Leader of the Pack

A woman quits her job to live her dream of being in the derby.

BOOKS

Coppage Keith. Roller Derby to RollerJam: The Authorized Story of an Unauthorized Sport.

Keith Coppage chronicles the game's beginnings and history, players and promoters.

Deford, Frank. Five Strides on the Banked Track: The Life and Times of the Roller Derby.

This behind-the-scenes look at the history of derby also details many of the famed skaters who were integral to the game's evolution.

Fitzpatrick, Jim. Roller Derby Classics...and More!

Former professional roller derby skater, referee, photographer, and fan, Fitzpatrick gives a glimpse into the world of historical banked-track mayhem.

Michelson, Herb. A Very Simple Game: The Story of Roller Derby.

This book covers roller derby's past, including profiles of historical skaters.

CREDITS

INDEX